Turning Your *Dream Business* into your BREAD & BUTTER

Recipes for Running a Successful Business from Scratch

ELLEN V. SPRINGER,
MBA, CPA

Marketing
Employees
Cash Flow

M·J
NEW YORK

Turning Your Dream Business Into Your Bread and Butter

Visit Ellen at www.RunASuccessfulBusiness.com
or email her at ESpringer@SpringerCPA.com

Paperback ISBN: 978-1-60037-223-0

Hardcover ISBN: 978-1-60037-224-7

eBook ISBN: 978-1-60037-225-4

Audio ISBN: 978-1-60037-226-1

Published by:

MORGAN · JAMES
THE ENTREPRENEURIAL PUBLISHER

Morgan James Publishing, LLC
1225 Franklin Ave. Ste 325
Garden City, NY 11530-1693
Toll Free 800-485-4943
www.MorganJamesPublishing.com

Cover & Interior Design by:
Heather Kirk
www.BrandedForSuccess.com
Heather@BrandedForSuccess.com

ACKNOWLEDGEMENTS

Elizabeth E.S. Hollander, Esquire, for inspiring and editing contributions.

J. Sam Johnson, CPA, Toccoa, Georgia for consulting and editing contributions.

John "Sandy" D. Sanders, Marketing specialist and consultant for his marketing contributions and encouragement.

Chad Massaker, Carceron Systems Group, LLC, Computer Consulting Firm, for technology expertise and editing contributions.

Dr Tarshia Stanley, Assistant Professor, English Department, Spelman College, Atlanta, Georgia, for editing contributions.

Cover Photo taken by Stephen H. Moore — Ace Photographer. SHMoore.com

For more information:
www.RunASuccessfulBusiness.com
www.SpringerCPA.com
www.LegacyWMI.com

A percentage of all proceeds are donated to the favorite charities of Ellen Springer.

DEDICATION

To every business owner,
may you be blessed with prosperity
and success with the
strategies in this book.

To my Heavenly Father,
for blessing me with
the knowledge and the words
to share with you.

To Mom and Dad,
Liz and Lee,
Sandy,
Sam and Chad
for believing in me
and encouraging me to
share my knowledge
through this book
so that I can make
a difference in
small business owners' lives.

Note From Author

The small business market segment needs a spokesperson to educate them on issues that affect them everyday. ***Turning Your Dream Business Into Your Bread and Butter: Recipes for Running a Successful Business from Scratch*** is the first in a series of books targeted to small business owners to explain in plain English, practical ways to set up and run their business more successfully. Examples of small business situations are presented and the strategies are applied to these businesses in each chapter.

The appendixes at the end of the book provide additional resources for websites, software, and reference materials and examples to assist you in applying the strategies outlined in this book.

Please write in this book and use it as a reference book through all the stages of your business. There are tables recapping the strategies at the end of each chapter, with page references and a column to apply to your business. Reading for knowledge is admirable, but to really learn and benefit from knowledge you need to apply it. I challenge you to apply it and benefit from you business success.

Visit my website **www.RunASuccessfulBusiness.com** for tax updates and bonuses available for the readers.

Table Of Contents

FOREWORD

There are no shortage of "how to" books on business. They are abundant. Perhaps, even overly abundant. The challenge is finding one that shares both the functional knowledge and the practical insights needed to start or maintain a small business. *Turning Your Dream Business Into Your Bread and Butter* is one such book.

Turning Your Dream Business Into Your Bread and Butter serves both as a "how-to guide" for those just starting businesses and as a reference guide for managers of established small businesses who need a refresher on addressing the fundamental challenges that they face.

By training and practice, Ellen Springer is an expert accountant. While her professional practice has expanded into the areas of financial planning and business consulting, she called upon her decades of accounting experience in the creation of this book. That background serves her well by providing the expertise to address the accounting, tax and financial issues that arise in most small businesses.

However, her background also provided the personal experiences, both as a small business owner and as an adviser to hundreds of small businesses, from which Ellen Springer fills this book with real-world examples. As such, the reader is treated to a survey of best (and in some cases worse) practices in small business management.

Turning Your Dream Business Into Your Bread and Butter walks the reader through the life cycle of a business from conception of the business model to a transfer in ownership.

After a brief introduction, Chapter 2 considers the development of an effective business plan. Chapters 3 and 4 address important issues in the legal structure of a business. While they consider the implications of such structures for tax liability, legal liability and corporate control, the more human concerns of the structure of the small business are also discussed.

Once the basic business plan is established and corporate structure established, the next a challenge is assembling the human and financial capital and selecting the business location with which to execute the business model. These steps are the topics of Chapters 5 through 8. Again, practical experience provides examples that warn the reader away from common pitfalls faced by other business owners.

Chapters 9 and 10 address important issues in information technology with a strong emphasis on the design and use of databases. Chapter 11 and 12 consider both traditional and Internet-based marketing. One could argue that the rise in Internet-based marketing has actually helped "level the playing field" between large and small businesses. Thus, the importance of this marketing channel for all businesses has increased.

Chapters 13 through 16 tour important issues in accounting systems and short-term financial management including managing cash flow and inventory, monitoring financial performance and determining the merits of buying versus leasing assets. In these chapters, Ellen Springer shows her uncommon ability to explain important accounting issues in a manner free of excessive business 'jargon."

Since no business can succeed without customers, it is appropriate that Chapter 17 addresses customer service. Here, the treatment emphasizes the importance of good communication with customers.

Of course, no business book written by a CPA would be complete without encouraging the business owner to consider investing in retirement plans and explaining the interaction with the Internal Revenue Service. These are the topics of Chapters 18 and 19. That the tax implications of various retirement programs can be addressed in a clear and accessible manner is a highlight of this section.

While some owners of small, closely-held businesses wish to transfer the entity on to a key employee or family members, others opt for selling the business. Chapter 20 surveys a variety of exit strategies. This section is particularly strong in its treatment of the financing and tax consequences of the purchase of a business.

This greatest return for this book will be for the reader who works through the chapters in order. At the end of each chapter, the reader is asked to review a checklist that summarizes the key actions and best practices from that chapter and apply them to their business.

While it is true that a seasoned business owner may benefit from reading key chapters when needed, the book is designed to flow through the life cycle of the business. Those readers who follow this framework will be rewarded with a systematic and rewarding treatment of starting and maintaining a successful small business.

Business writings are frequently dominated by "fads" that are short-lived and unproductive. *Turning Your Dream Business Into Your Bread and Butter* is a collection of practical, time-tested, but still contemporary, lessons for the small business owner. Those who consume it will be better managers for having done so.

Roger Tutterow, Ph.D.
Dean & Professor
Stetson School of Business & Economics
Mercer University
Atlanta & Macon, GA

INTRODUCTION

"The biggest adventure you can ever take is to live the life of your dreams."

Oprah Winfrey, O Magazine
U.S. Actress & Television Talk Show Host (1954 -)

Do you have a dream business — either in your mind or already running — that you want to turn into a successful reality? Many business owners do.

Everyone goes into business for one of several reasons. Many "bread winners" go into business for themselves to provide for their families. Others are currently doing something that they love to do but are tired of someone else making money from their hard efforts. Or, they believe that they can do it better and make more money for themselves. Still others come up with a million dollar idea that will solve a need in business or in the world. As a dear friend once told me, "One person's problem is another person's opportunity."

Running your dream business requires a number of different skill sets. You need sales and marketing skills, an optimistic outlook, and the ability to turn every contact into a marketing opportunity. The ability to analyze numbers and understand the story your financial statements are telling you is important, as well as the ability to effectively manage employees and systems, understand the big picture, and plan for the future. It is unrealistic to expect that one person can possess all of the skills necessary to run a successful business. The good news is that it's not necessary to possess every last skill to achieve your dream.

I have a son with an extremely high IQ and learning disabilities in reading and spelling. He has struggled in school, and at times the teachers didn't want to provide him with the accommodations that he needed as they equated learning disabilities with a low IQ. In addition to this, he doesn't want anyone to know anything is "wrong" with him and so he tries to do the work without any accommodations and sometimes doesn't do as well. He recently asked me, "Mom, assume that I manage to get a college degree, how will I ever be able to do any job completely by myself?" I realized that he was living in fear that his ultimate goal — the job — was something he would be unable to do without help. I told him that no one could do 100% of their job by themselves. The challenge for most people is figuring out the 70 to 75% that they can do. Then they can cover the other 25 to 30% by hiring or teaming up with someone who can do the part that they couldn't. He was so relieved and has since agreed to tackle the next college course. My son was lucky. He had a testing report that told us his strengths and the areas where he needed someone else to help. We were able to develop a strategy because we were aware of the problem areas and thus could overcome the fear and the potential for failure.

I realize that many business owners have this same fear standing in the way of their dream. How can you obtain all of the information required to start and be successful in business? I have had some business owners tell me if they had known what was really required to start their business, they never would have done it. Others have said that they wish they had hired more people who possessed the skill sets they lacked sooner, thus preventing painful struggles.

Sometimes the most successful businesses are those filled with people of different skill sets, teaming up and starting a business together, rather than the one person approach. There are challenges to working with people who see the world differently, but there are also great rewards.

Whatever your reason for starting your new business, it is okay not to know everything and okay not to possess all of the skill sets that you will need. It is important to learn your strengths and to recognize the areas where you will need assistance. Recognize the need to hire or team up with those individuals who will help you be successful.

I recently climbed Amicalola Falls, in North Georgia, and was fascinated as I stood on the bridge at the very top. On one side was calm water. It was clear and looked as though it was barely moving. On the other side was a raging waterfall. The water traveled at a high speed, pummeled rocks, and gave off an abundance of energy that made the most spectacular sight. What happened? What changed the calm water? Was it the same water, I wondered? I offer to you that the difference in the water was the change in its environment. All the things surrounding the water and acting upon it, the rocks, the drop, gravity, made the difference.

This same principle is at work in business. We don't have to know everything there is to know about business. We just need to surround ourselves with the right ingredients to create the energy and atmosphere needed to generate a great business.

I offer this book to you if you are ready to be successful in your dream business. It is full of my recipes and contains all the right ingredients to insure you reach your goals. Please use the checklists at the end of each chapter to right down how the strategies can be applied to your dream business.

I congratulate you and wish you the very best so that you can "live the life of your dreams."

Please note that there are references in this book to tax information for the tax years 2006 and 2007, in some cases 2006 rates and limits will apply with extensions. Updated tax information for future years can be downloaded from www.RunASuccessfulBusiness.com. Visit the website for more resources to run a successful business.

CHAPTER 1
My Bread & Butter

"The history of the world is the record of a man in quest for his daily bread and butter."

Hendrick Willem Van Loon

Many business owners refer to their business as "My Bread and Butter." Why do they do this? The business is the place where the money is generated to be able to buy the bread and butter for the family. Also, the products or services that are the mainstay of the business and provide the income stream to keep the business operating, are sometimes referred to as "the bread and butter" of the business. In this book we are going to explore the basics of setting up your business the right way so that you can enjoy the bread and butter that will be generated for you, your family and for your employees through the business.

Owning your own business is both scary and exciting at the same time. Throughout my 25-plus years working as a CPA with clients in business I have found that most people want to start their own business because: 1) They have a new idea and they want to be the one to reap the benefits; 2) They are tired of other people making money on their ideas or efforts; 3) They feel that they can run the business better than their employer; or 4) They inherited or received a lump sum of money and they want to finally pursue a dream.

However, going into business is not for everyone. There are some people who shouldn't own their own business. They need the discipline of corporate America dictating what time to be at work, what time to leave, and all the other components of performing their job. If you are going to have your own business you have to be a self-starter, willing to work whenever and however long it takes. Instead of one boss you now have many bosses, and they are called your clients or customers. You will be wearing many hats and need to be willing to put the kind of hours into the business that will make it competitive with larger companies.

I once invited a client who was considering starting his own business to come to my office for a conference. I showed him into my conference room where I had hats sitting on each chair around the conference table. I asked him to take a seat at the head of the table and to put on the hat labeled "President". I began to describe the activities that came along with the title. I listed the things for which he would be responsible including providing a vision for the company, managing the managers and taking full responsibility for the success or failure of the company. I had him move to the next chair and put on the hat labeled, "Sales and Marketing". I listed for him all the duties that particular job entailed. They included developing the marketing plan, designing the letterhead, creating the logo, advertising in newspapers, and on radio/tv, negotiating ad contracts and deals, developing and motivating the sales force, and making sure the invoices and statements were mailed each month. In the next chair he put on the hat labeled "Customer Service." This position included handling customer complaints, answering questions for clients or customers, unraveling customer misunderstandings and training staff to work with clients or customers.

I went on to list the job descriptions for Personnel, Accounting, and Inventory Management He sat there trying to absorb all of the different tasks and roles that he was going to assume by starting his own business. Even though he might hire different people for each function, he was ultimately responsible and needed to be clear about what was involved with each "hat." The bottom line was that he needed more information to be able to be successful in running his business because he had underestimated the time it was going to take to learn and to manage this new business.

It is very rare that any one person can possess all of the skill sets that are required for the "hats" that I have described above. Thus, for small business owners this is probably the biggest challenge that they face. They don't have money to spare to purchase the various skills and expertise that they are going to need so the owner tries to fill in the gaps. Sometimes the owner is successful but sometimes he or she is not.

"The Buck Stops Here" is an important concept for the business owner to understand. As the owner you are the ultimate manager of all of the activities of the business either personally or through other employees. The best description of management that I have heard was described in one of my graduate classes: The act of managing is similar to having a handful of playdough and squeezing it. You have most of it inside your hand, a little bit squeezes out between the fingers. Then you let go and get another hold and squeeze again. The same thing happens as you squeeze again, you have most of it inside your hand, but a little bit squeezes out between your fingers. However the pieces that escape with each successive squeeze are not exactly the same pieces that escaped before. Managing is the process of squeezing and letting go, squeezing and letting go, etc. and hoping that you hold every piece of the playdough at some point. The moments where you've handled all the dough could be during the month, quarter or year.

Taking time to obtain the necessary information to set up your business properly will save you valuable time and hard earned money. You can either: buy knowledge and learn from it, or you can learn from experience. Sometimes this is called the "the school of hard knocks" method. Either way, knowledge is expensive not only in time, but mental strain and money.

I have had numerous clients who didn't take time to plan and learn, say, "If I had known what was involved in starting this business, I never would have started it." I have reviewed with some clients that the number of hours that they are working compared to the amount of income that they are making, is less than minimum wage. They would be better off working for someone else and making substantially more money with less headaches and less stress. Sometimes you determine through the planning process that your venture will not make enough money to provide the bread and butter for your family and your employees.

Because it takes so much effort and sacrifice for a new business owner and his/her family to start a new business, it is so very important that the business be something that they are passionate about and really, really enjoy so that they can make the commitment to do whatever it takes to be successful. Otherwise, they can't be successful, because they won't put the time and effort into it to make it successful. Remember, you have to be willing to go the extra mile, but the good news is that it is never crowded!

Let's assume that you have prepared and you decided to start your business, the first year is the hardest because you don't know what the next month will bring. Will you have sales? What new thing will happen that you had not anticipated? You don't know what you don't know. There are still so many things to learn.

The second year there will be some repeats and a few more things that are unknowns. But at least you know that you made it through the first year and the lulls in sales in certain months are welcomed so that you are able to catch up on the mounting tasks of a business owner.

The second year you learn to ask more questions, to be less trusting and put more value on advice. As a general rule, I would rather be someone's second CPA because they appreciate the value of professional advice and actually do what I recommend.

I have noticed over the years that clients become more willing as they grow and learn with their business to make the hard decisions. Terminating a nice employee, reducing overhead, closing a favorite line of business, and expanding into new markets are all examples of those hard decisions. Sometimes deciding to trust an instinct or gut feeling and going for it are decisions that are just as hard to make. Doing the hard thing is many times the same thing as doing the right thing. I have told many a client to trust their instincts. Nine times out of ten when I don't trust mine, I falter and I make the wrong decision.

Another reason for taking the time to become educated before setting up your business is that a large percentage of businesses fail in the first five years of operation. The rate is somewhere between 60 and 80%. That is a large number and you want to take steps early so that you will not be included in these statistics. With this percentage so high, isn't it worth it to take time to invest in your future and become prepared?

In each chapter of this book we are going to explore the basic needs of your business through the recipes for success and I will assist you in determining the bread and butter of your business. Make sure that after each chapter you complete the worksheets and checklists and list the decisions that you have made and the tasks that have been accomplished so that when you complete the book you are well on your way having a successful business.

CHAPTER 2
Menu for Success: Business Plan & Budgets

Trevor has worked for a successful sports bar for two years and dreams of opening his own sports bar near his home. He visits his local banker and the banker asks for his business plan but Trevor doesn't have one. The banker explains that he can't loan money on a dream, he must have something that he can take to the loan committee to show the potential success of the business and the ability to repay the loan. He tells him to write his business plan and come back to see him.

Tell a story. Your business starts with a dream, an idea or concept, but you must develop it. Your business plan is the menu for success. The business plan should tell a story. It should describe how you are going to set up your business, explain what you are going to sell and to whom, as well as explain how you are going to promote your product and services.

Most businesses don't plan to fail, they fail to plan. Preparing business plans and budgets enables the business owner to create goals both initially and annually and then establish the game plans to accomplish them. Most business owners are not comfortable tackling this task and their business fails because of it. This chapter gives the business owner strategies to apply and practical reasons for preparing these documents.

Planning prevents you from starting a business that won't work. By working through a business plan before you start your business, you are forced to review all aspects of the business and determine whether you can make the money that you need to make before you invest the time, energy and money into it. This will prevent disappointments and the loss of money that the family could use in other ways.

You are more committed to something that is in writing. An idea in your head is not concrete and it is hard for someone else to understand and visualize. If you have to put it on paper, you have to develop the idea more fully and describe it so someone else can understand. Your idea looks different on paper and can be fine tuned as you think through all of the different areas of the idea. Someone else can ask questions and provide guidance in making the idea a reality. When you start the business, you can go back to the plan for guidance as you reach decision points along the way.

Banks and Venture Capitalist require business plans. Most lenders and investors won't consider investing money in your business unless you have a business plan. If you are figuring out your business as you go, you are less likely to be successful. You may not have enough time to adjust to the changes in the marketplace if you don't have a game plan in place. By taking the time to develop a business plan and financial projections you can identify the bumps in the road in terms of cash flow and have a better idea of the cash required to start and grow your business.

Utilize focus groups. Some things are unknown when preparing a business plan, especially with new products or services that don't have a track record. You may not know how the public will receive this new idea, concept or product. One way to reduce the unknowns is to do focus groups. Select representatives from various demographic groups, have the participants sign non-disclosure statements, and introduce the idea, concept or product and record their responses. If a large enough sample is selected, then assumptions can be made about the demographic population at large. If the responses are not favorable, you can avoid investing in something that may not be marketable or may be too far ahead of it's time.

Money causes relationships to suffer. Money does strange things to relationships. When you borrow money from friends, family and relatives, the relationships will change. In terms of your business, if you don't respect the rules as far as money is concerned, your relationships will suffer. I have seen more families and friendships destroyed because of businesses failing and the promises made concerning the business which were made but not kept.

Parts of a business plan. What should a business plan include? The parts of a business plan include: Executive Summary, Company Summary, Market analysis Summary, Strategy and Implementation Summary, Management Summary and Financial Plan and Projections.

The Executive Summary should grab the reader. The executive summary summarizes the type of business, the location and the overall plans of the business in sales and profitability and timetable. This section needs to catch the reader's attention and sell them on the idea by explaining the reasons for being in this business. Sub-sections may include: objectives, mission and the keys to success. Objectives may describe what makes this business unique and special and its goals for success. The mission describes the purpose of the business and the ultimate goal. The keys to success highlight the expertise that will set the business apart and make it successful.

The Company Summary should highlight the strengths of the company and the ownership. The Company Summary should describe the key elements of the company concepts that will make it successful. The type of entity and the ownership and capitalization goals are described. If this is an expansion of an existing business, then a history of the existing company should be included. The successes of the existing company including highlighted financial numbers are also presented. The reasons for the expansion should be outlined as well as the reasons for considering it.

Market Analysis Summary describes the competition and overall marketplace. The Market Analysis summary describes the competition and industry in a particular locale over a period of time and the expectations for the future. A section on the competition should be included with a description of how they will affect your business and how you will compete with them.

Strategy and Implementation summary should outline how to get there from here. Strategy and Implementation summary outlines the overall marketing plan, including the pricing, promotion, and marketing goals. The sales strategy and forecasts by month and product line are usually included. Milestones and significant goals are also disclosed.

Management Summary describes the management team. The Management Summary includes an organizational chart, the qualifications of each member of the management team and their experience in the industry, areas that need to be covered outside of the management team, and the overall personnel plan.

The Financial Plan quantifies the goals and concepts. The financial plan is where every goal is quantified and translated into dollars and cents. Important assumptions and key financial indicators are listed. A break-even analysis should be included to determine the minimum amount of sales required to break-even. See Chapter 14, Managing Cash Flow, for more information on break-even analysis. Sample profit and loss statements are available on the Internet for various industries to use as a guide to prepare your financial projections. Projections of profit and loss by month, balance sheet by month and cash flow by month should be included. Determine business ratios and compare them to industry averages.

The Financial plan is the basis for the budget. Your financial plan in the business plan becomes your first year's budget. I recommend inputting the budget into the accounting software to compare against actual revenue and expenses each month.

Hire a CPA for the financial projections. If the financial projections are not your expertise, work with a CPA to assist you so that you don't forget key expenses and capital expenditures that will occur in the business. The CPA will discuss the assumptions with you and prepare the financial projections for your business plan.

Be realistic and be conservative. It is best to underestimate revenue projections and overestimate expense projections in your financial projections. Sometimes three projections are prepared: worst case scenario, most realistic and best case scenario. This allows for ranges to be considered by the lenders and the owners.

Software programs for business plans. There are business plan software programs that walk you through the process with a series of questions. These help you with processes that are unfamiliar to you and assist you in preparing a basic business plan. They may not allow for unusual situations, but can provide a guide for the areas that need to be addressed in the plan.

If Trevor will take the time to put on paper the business plan for his new sports bar and why he believes he will be successful, then he can be just that. If he prepares realistic financial plans that show that he can pay the bank back any money he borrows, then the bank may lend him the money and allow him to live his dream. But it won't happen it he doesn't take the first step toward developing his business plan.

BUSINESS PLANS & BUDGETS CHECKLIST

	Strategy	Page Ref #	Application To Your Business
1.	Tell a story	15	
2.	Most businesses don't plan to fail they fail to plan	15	
3.	Planning prevents you from starting a business that won't work	15	
4.	You are more committed to something that is in writing	16	
5.	Banks and Venture Capitalist require business plans	16	
6.	Utilize focus groups	16	
7.	Money causes relationships to suffer	16	
8.	Parts of a business plan	17	
9.	The executive summary should grab the reader	17	
10.	The company summary should highlight the strengths of the company and the ownership	17	
11.	Market analysis summary describes the competition and overall marketplace	17	

	Strategy	Page Ref #	Application To Your Business
12.	Strategies and implementation summary should outline how to get there from here	17	
13.	Management summary describes the management team	18	
14.	Financial Plan quantifies the goals and concepts	18	
15.	Financial plan is basis for the budget	18	
16.	Hire a CPA for the financial projections	18	
17.	Be realistic and be conservative	18	
18.	Software programs for business plans	18	

CHAPTER 3
Choosing Your Legal Entity

Why is choosing your legal entity such a "big deal"? What if you own a restaurant and someone choked and died on a bone that was in the fish that was served and you did not have an entity that gave you limited liability and all of your family assets were now at risk? What if you were a C Corporation and all of your assets were sold and then you found out that you now have to pay taxes on the same income twice through the corporation and then when you liquidate the corporation? What if your corporate papers stated that your corporation was suppose to be an S Corporation. You meet with your tax advisor at the end of the year, and find out that you were suppose to have filed an election with the Internal Revenue Service earlier in the year. Because this election wasn't filed the corporation is actually a C Corporation now with taxes due at the corporate level. Why didn't you meet with your tax advisor before finalizing the choice of legal entity? Wouldn't it be great to know the questions to ask before you set up your business to avoid these costly mistakes?

Five basic choices of legal entities. There are five basic choices in choosing the legal entity for your business, Sole Proprietorship, Partnership, Regular Corporation, S Corporation, and Limited Liability Company. Before we explore each one, there are a number of factors that should be considered in the decision: Legal Liability, Transfer of Ownership, Life of the Entity, Tax Filing, Taxation of the Income, Administrative and Legal Costs, Fringe Benefits, and Exit Strategy.

A Sole Proprietorship. A Sole Proprietorship does not require extensive legal costs up front. You can begin operating by printing business cards with your new business name and collecting income and paying expenses. I recommend registering your business name with the county or province in which you operate and if you have a special logo or tag line, then consider registering it as a trademark to protect it. With a Sole Proprietorship there is unlimited liability for the owner. Insurance can be purchased to protect the family assets, but if the owner can not purchase enough insurance or if the risk is too great to the family, another entity with limited liability should be considered. With this entity, the business does not continue with the death of the owner. Therefore, licenses, identification numbers and names must be reapplied for under the new owner or beneficiary's name.

The sole proprietor does not have to maintain a "set of books" for his or her business, therefore, the owner doesn't have to open and maintain a separate bank account or a formal set of books. Sales and expense receipts by category can be added up at the end of the year and recorded on the Schedule C on the personal return to determine the net income and related taxes. The tax return filing process is the simplest of the entities, as additional schedules are added to the personal tax return instead of a separate set of tax returns being required for the business. If you don't have employees, you don't have to apply for an employer identification number or other payroll tax numbers.

If the unlimited liability exposure and the lack of continuation of the business at the death of the owner are important issues, then this is not the entity to choose. If you want ease of operation and the least amount of paperwork, and you don't have to protect a name or logo etc., and you want the lowest legal costs to start the business then this might be the entity to choose.

The Partnership. The Partnership is similar to the Sole Proprietorship as the general partners have unlimited liability. You must have at least two people as owners to have a partnership. If the partnership has limited partners, then the liability is limited for them alone. A limited partnership must have at least one general partner and the general partner will not have limited liability. Sometimes that general partner is a corporation to provide some form of limited liability with another layer for that general partner.

There will be more legal costs up front with a Partnership and a tailored partnership agreement should be prepared by an attorney. The partnership agreement should outline the income split between the partners, the equity required to be contributed to the partnership by each partner, the termination of a partner, the death of a partner, the entrance of a new partner, non-compete issues and the termination of the partnership.

The partnership is a "flow-through" or "pass-through" entity and thus does not pay income taxes, but passes all income and certain separate expenses through to the partners. The various income, expense and tax credit information is "passed-through" and reported at the individual partner level. The partnership files a Form 1065 and Schedule K-1s are provided to each partner to give them the information that should be recorded on their respective tax returns. An individual partner will record the information from the Schedule K-1 on their personal Form 1040 and related schedules. Each partner is taxed on his or her proportionate share of income based on the percentage outlined in the partnership agreement. If there is more than one owner, the administration of the business can be divided between the owners so that the burden is not entirely on one person.

C Corporation. Many small business owners choose to form a corporation to protect their personal assets from creditor claims. A regular corporation, sometimes referred to as a "C" Corporation, limits liability to the shareholders. To obtain this limited liability, Articles of Incorporation must be filed with the Secretary of State in your state and usually an attorney prepares these. Provided the shareholder does not personally guarantee the debt of the corporation, the shareholder is limited to loosing the investment in the stock of the company to creditor claims. Personal assets are therefore protected from creditors. The corporation's life is unlimited and does not terminate with the death of one or more of its shareholders. A corporation is a separate legal entity and must have a separate bank account and assets titled in its name. A corporation is also required to have a set of books and records to support and record the transactions of the entity. These books and records are used to file the corporation's Form 1120 and it pays taxes using the corporate tax rates as a separate taxpayer from the shareholders. If the shareholders are paid a dividend from the profits of the company, then the shareholders pay taxes on the dividends. Therefore, there is double taxation for the same corporate profits, taxed at the corporate level and taxed again at the individual level when paid out as dividends.

Another double taxation event occurs if the assets are sold at the corporate level, then taxes are due and when the assets are distributed to the shareholders upon dissolution of the corporation taxes are again due at the shareholder level. Eligible fringe benefits paid for a shareholder-employee are deductible by the corporation and not income to the shareholder-employee. In summary, a regular corporation has limited liability to the shareholders, fringe benefits for shareholder-employees, but it is a separate taxpayer with potential double taxation issues.

S Corporation. Another entity that provides limited liability but is also a pass-through entity for taxes is the S Corporation. It is a regular corporation for liability protection but an election must be filed with the Internal Revenue Service within two and one-half months from the inception or the beginning of a tax year in order to be recognized as an S Corporation for tax purposes. This election can be terminated voluntarily by the shareholders or involuntarily if the corporation no longer qualifies to maintain its "S" status. As long as it is an S Corporation, in general, the profits are taxed at the individual level and not at the corporate level. A Form 1120S is filed with the Internal Revenue Service and a Schedule K-1 is provided to each shareholder to use to record their information on their individual tax returns. Therefore, the double taxation is eliminated with both the dividend payments and the sale of the company assets (provided it has always been an S Corporation or has been an S Corporation for at least ten years).

Another tax benefit is that the S Corporation can distribute profits to their shareholders and the profits are only taxed at the shareholder level. This distribution of profits is not subject to self-employment taxes at the shareholder level. Only salaries paid to shareholder/employees are subject to Social Security and Medicare taxes. Sometimes business owners become greedy and refuse to take salaries and try to avoid the Social Security and Medicare taxes by paying only distributions. The IRS upon reviewing the transactions of the business can reclassify all of the business owner's distributions as salary subject to the Social Security and Medicare taxes. So be reasonable with the split between salary and distributions. An attorney will probably need to set up the corporation and I recommend a buy-sell agreement to be drafted and signed at the beginning of the Honeymoon phase of being in business together. Don't leave the future in the hands of someone else.

A set of books and records are also required to be maintained by the corporation. A corporation is held to a higher standard of record keeping than a sole proprietorship. Fringe benefits for a more than 2% shareholder are not deductible by the corporation and are therefore income to the shareholder/employee. It is easy to transfer stock ownership and the corporation will continue even with the death of one or more shareholders. If one of the shareholders wants to withdraw from the business and take assets with him or her, a taxable event will be triggered and taxes will be due, even though the assets have not been sold for cash.

A Limited Liability Company. Another entity that has limited liability to its owners and members is The Limited Liability Company (LLC). It can be taxed as a pass-through partnership or as a regular corporation. The tax benefit is derived with the partnership tax status. A single person can also be an LLC and file as a sole proprietorship for taxes with Schedule C and SE on the personal tax return but enjoy the limited liability protection of a corporation. Therefore, a complete set of LLC federal and state tax returns is not required for an individual, single member LLC. If there is more than one member or owner a partnership return, Form 1065 with related schedules is required to be filed. A schedule K-1 should be prepared to provide the partner/member with the necessary information to be reported on his/her personal return. The LLC is probably the best entity with not only the limited liability protection but it is the easiest tax wise when the members want to split up the assets and do something else. In general, the partners may withdraw assets from the LLC and not incur a taxable event until the member sells the asset(s).

If your business could potentially threaten someone's life you need to have limited liability from the first day of your business. Examples of industries that I believe should have limited liability are, food preparation or food product sales, construction, and transportation by car, truck, boat or plane.

Someone could die from eating the food that was prepared, sold, or distributed by your company. The construction industry (including residential, commercial, general or sub-contracting) is one of the most important businesses to insure. Anyone in any of your buildings could be the victim of fire, electrocution, building collapse, etc. If you are in the transportation business or have employees who are on the road servicing clients or customers you need to limit your liability.

Every company should have liability insurance but there are limits to policies and limiting your liability with corporations, limited partnerships and limited liability companies provides additional protection for personal assets.

If you desire to limit your liability and want to receive a salary with payroll taxes withheld and without the corporation paying taxes on the net income, then an S Corporation should be your choice. If you plan to have inventories and receivables that are substantial and you want to grow your business with the least amount of taxes in the short term then you might choose a C Corporation. However remember with C Corporations that the double taxation issue at dissolution must be considered.

You may choose to be a Sole Proprietor for reasons which include: the business is brand new, you don't know how much money you will make, you can insure for any liability concerns, and you want to keep it simple and not file separate tax returns. You can incorporate at any time if your concerns or goals change. I still recommend that the business have a separate bank account and a set of books so that the business owner can monitor the business activities and compare them to the business plan and budget.

Sometimes business owners incorporate to be on the approved vendor list with a particular large corporation. Some corporations require everyone they work with to be a corporation with certain limits of liability insurance. Some business owners want to appear to be larger or more sophisticated with their customers and having the corporate name gives that impression.

A Limited Liability Company can have different legal entities as partners. An individual, a partnership, another LLC and a Corporation can be partners. This allows for different types of entities to come together to form strategic alliances and market as one entity.

Limited Liability Company's and Limited Partnerships are sometimes used to transfer interest in businesses to the children of the business owner or owners. The management agreement or limited partnership agreement can dictate that the equity ownership percentages are different from the income or loss percentages. HoweveroweH, an S Corporation's equity ownership and income or loss percentage is the same as the percentage of the shareholder's ownership in the S Corporation during the year. The Managing Member or General Partner can control the entity and run the business for the rest of the members and partners regardless of the percentage ownership. S corporations have to elect a Board of Directors that hire the management to run the business.

There are a number of choices in legal entities and this decision will probably be one of the most important that you will make in setting up your company, please take the time to obtain legal and tax advice before finalizing your decision. Ask questions and request "what if" scenarios from your advisors. What if I want to add a partner? What if my partner and I want to split up? What if I die? What if I want to sell my business? What if I want to bring one of my children into the business? What if I am sued?

Once the decision is made to set up your legal entity, follow through with all of the paperwork. Make sure that the stock certificates are signed and issued and put in a safe place. Sign the Organizational Minutes and the Management or Partnership Agreement and sign the buy/sell agreements and put your copy in a safe, secure place. Consider funding the buy/sell agreements with life insurance on the lives of the owners so that you will have the cash to buy out the owner who has died. This also provides your former partner's family which much needed cash.

I have observed many misunderstandings between owners who destroyed businesses and relationships because the buy/sell agreements were never completed and each party remembered something different in the verbal agreement. The lawyers are the ones who make the money if this happens at this point so please avoid such situations. Do it right the first time and give your business the best opportunity for success.

Preparing all of the paperwork and executing it to set up the business is very important. It is also important to honor the entity that you have set up and follow the rules to continue to protect the business. If you elect to set up a C or an S Corporation or a Limited Liability Company these are separate legal entities from you and separate bank accounts which need to be set up. Business transactions should be made through these business accounts. If you deposit income into your personal account or pay personal expenses out of the business account, the line becomes blurred and the limited liability protection might be challenged. Document the loans between the owners and the business. When in doubt as to what to do, compare your business to a well known publicly traded company and ask yourself what you would you do if your business was that company and how would you structure the transaction and document it.

You can change legal entities after your business is started. You can incorporate a sole proprietorship or a partnership. You can elect to be taxed as an S Corporation when you have been a C Corporation and vice versus. To become an S Corporation and you have an existing C Corporation, an election must be filed with the IRS within 2 1/5 months after the beginning of the tax year effective for that tax year. If you involuntarily revoke an S Election in the middle of a tax year multiple tax returns may be required during the middle of a tax year, taxes may be due, tax consequences may be triggered and elections may need to be made so consult your tax advisor before making any changes.

Choosing your legal entity is a "big deal" and should be researched as it applies to your business, industry and family situation. The best decision you can make will depend upon the time and effort you put into researching all your options.

COMPARISON OF FIVE BASIC BUSINESS ENTITIES

	Sole Proprietorship	Partnership	C Corporation	S Corporation	Limited Liability Company
Legal Liability	Unlimited	Unlimited for General Partners Limited for Limited Partners	Limited	Limited	Limited
Transfer of Ownership	Difficult	Difficult unless provisions in partnership agreement	Unlimited	Unlimited	Varies
Life of Entity	Life of Proprietor	Limited unless provisions in partnership agreement	Stock Transfer	Stock Transfer	Varies
Tax Filing*	Schedule C with Form 1040	Form 1065 with Distribution of Schedule K-1	Form 1120	Form 1120S	Form 1065 if taxed as Partnership Form 1120 if taxed as Corporation
Taxation of Income	Directly to Proprietor	Directly to Partners	Corporation pays taxes	Taxed directly to shareholders	If taxed as partnership directly to partners If taxed as corporation corporation

* State Tax Returns may be required in addition to federal returns

CHAPTER 4
Partnership & Buy/Sell Agreements

Charles and Forrest formed a partnership to make and sell toys to stores around the country. Charles had designed several new toys but wasn't comfortable selling them to potential buyers. Forrest was a salesman and enjoyed selling but didn't know how to fix or design anything. The partnership appeared to be ideal, but after a few months Charles and Forrest started to argue every time they talked. It turned out that Charles thought he was going to receive a royalty fee from the sale of each of his patents on the new toys before the profits were split between them. Forrest thought that they were splitting everything 50/50 and didn't know about a royalty fee. Charles also planned to make monthly distributions and Forrest wanted distributions paid twice a month. Charles decided to have his two children share in his interest, while Forrest did not want to work with his children. They jumped into the partnership and did not have anything in writing to describe the compensation, distributions, or the right to sell their interest. Now their partnership is on the verge of a breakdown.

Partner versus owner versus shareholder. In this chapter, when I refer to a "partner," I am referring to an owner, whether they are technically a partner or shareholder, etc. Partnerships have "partners." Corporations have "shareholders." Partners and shareholders are both owners. See Chapter 3, *Choosing Your Legal Entity*, for more information on each of these entities and to help you chose which one is best for your business.

Something must be gained by each partner for them to stay together. On the surface, it looks like Charles and Forrest have formed an ideal partnership, with each having strengths in different areas. Charles likes to invent and design toys and Forrest likes to sell. This is the fundamental basis for this partnership, and as long as Charles needs someone to sell his toys and Forrest wants to sell them, they both benefit from the partnership. When one partner no longer needs the other partner or stops believing that the other partner is of value, the partnership will fall apart.

Misunderstandings occur when details are not discussed ahead of time. Misunderstandings occur when details are not worked out in advance and a partner finds out that his understanding of something which matters to him is different from the other partner's. Hopefully the partners can sit down and discuss the conflict and resolve it, or arrive at a compromise to which both parties will agree.

Have a partner or be in business by yourself?: It is a trade off. There are only 24 hours in a day. Believe me, I try every day to squeeze more in and I can't. Partners can complicate your life, or they can make it simpler and easier. When you are in business for yourself, you don't have anyone to relieve you when you want to take time off. Vacations other than long weekends are difficult and even then you have to be on call by phone for questions and emergencies. With a partner, you at least have someone who can deal with the questions and emergencies in your absence.

Partners may not do it exactly the way that you would. Your partner may deal with a situation, but he or she may not do it exactly the way that you would. A partnership involves allowing the partner to do it his or her way. You need only be sure that the end result is desirable and nothing illegal or immoral occurs.

The things that make you successful are the very things that can drive you crazy. Charles can't sell his toys and he probably doesn't have a personality that lends itself to selling naturally. Forrest has a natural ability to sell and doesn't have a clue about designing and building toys. These are very different people and although they will have a hard time understanding each other's needs and perspectives in their area of the business, they need each other to be successful. It is important for partners to each recognize that they would have a difficult time being as successful without the other.

Respect and accept one another's differences. Being different is OK. Acknowledging this is very important in a partnership.

Sometimes a third-party mediator can help. When partners are very different and recognize that they need to work together but don't know how to communicate, a third-party mediator can help. I once had a business client that had four owners but they rarely talked with one another. I delivered their financial statements each month and the owners met with me in the conference room to go over the statements. I would ask each of them questions about their area of responsibility and they would respond and the others would listen and ask me questions and I would repeat them, etc. It worked. They became multi-millionaires when I assisted them with the sale of their business. Even though they were not able to communicate directly with one another, they recognized the need for a third-party mediator and set their pride aside for the success of the company. Don't let pride get in the way of being successful and making money.

Outside board members or an advisory board. Another way to settle differences of opinion in the way the business is run or about the direction the business should move is to have one or more outside board members on your board of directors. This takes the emotion out of decisions. Presentations are made to these independent members and objective opinions are requested. One of my clients that formed a 50/50 partnership added an outside board member to break ties and for outside input. They both agreed that they would agree to be bound by the outside board member's vote on issues which they disagreed. This allowed their partnership to survive even they didn't always agree. Sometimes "what is best for the business" is lost in the partner's struggle to have their way or to win an argument.

Agree to disagree. When the issue doesn't involve much money and/or when the values of a partner are not compromised, agreeing to disagree is a form of agreement and it is OK. Just because you are partners does not mean that you each give up your identity or opinions, or that you have to agree on everything. A partnership where both parties agreed on everything would be very boring and might not be successful. It is disagreement and new ideas that generate even better ideas from the synergy of discussion and the exploration of all aspects of an idea. Sometimes disagreeing can be a good thing.

Be yourself. It won't work for the long term if you try to be someone who you are not, just to please your partner. You should honor yourself and be yourself. Trying to be someone who you are not will eventually cause you to either blow up at the other partner or cause your health to suffer. I tried to stay in a partnership that I was uncomfortable with because I was determined to make it work. I developed stomach problems after awhile from the stress of the situation. You should be respectful, yet honest with your partner. If you are unhappy, your partner probably is too.

More ideas. When there are multiple partners more ideas can be generated and explored than if there is only one person. Some owners use employees to gain additional ideas. Keep in mind, however, that employees and owners tend to have different mindsets. Although additional ideas may be generated, the concern and care with having the business be successful is usually not the same with an employee as it is with an owner. By the same token, that difference in perspective could be an asset in some respects. It could help to improve areas such as customer service (See Chapter 17).

Built-in sounding board. With partners, you can discuss customers and situations, and bounce ideas off one another. It is less lonely and can alleviate worry concerning a decision or recommendation to a customer. I have had many sole owners tell me that not having someone as a sounding board is the one thing that they miss about being in business without a partner. They feel like they are all alone and face all of the business decisions without the benefit of a peer with whom to discuss important decisions.

Divide and conquer tasks. With more than one owner, tasks can be divided and conquered between partners. You can access each other's strengths, and assign tasks based on one another's abilities. The partner with a specific skill can complete tasks requiring this skill easily. A partner without the necessary skill will struggle or avoid tasks that require this skill and the business will suffer.

One partner may be able to sell, like Forrest; another partner may have the skills in accounting or managing employees. If you have to do everything, it may not get done and your business may suffer.

Partnership and operating agreement. A partnership and operating agreement should address such things as when distributions will be paid, the responsibility of each functional partner, and which decisions require all partners to vote. Committing the partnership entity to borrow money usually requires all partners to vote. Hiring employees may or may not require all partners to vote. Determining how often the partnership will have formal partner meetings and when financial statements and tax returns will be prepared should be included in the operating agreement. I recommend that you complete the monthly financial statements within 30 days of each month's end. I also recommend that the partnership or corporate tax return be completed by the IRS specified due date, unless the partners agrees to an extension. Special compensation arrangements with one or more partners should be included as well. For example, the royalty fee that Charles thought he was going to be paid should have been included in a partnership agreement. A managing partner sometimes is paid an extra draw for the added management responsibility. Include all operational items that could potentially cause conflict between partners in the partnership and operating agreement.

Don't compete with your partner. It is important not to compete with your partner. If you believe that you have to do everything as well or better than your partner then sooner or later one of you will be ready to call it quits. It is OK to for each of you to be better at different things. The beauty of a partnership is that you have different skill sets not that you each have the same skill sets and are equally as good in everything. Your business should be better because of that.

Partners can make more money when sharing overhead. If both partners are in the same business, teaming up under the same roof and sharing resources will allow each of them to make more money. This is especially true in service businesses. It takes the same amount of resources to have one business principal as to have several principals. Instead of each partner paying for their own, computer servers, telephone systems, receptionists, reception rooms, conference rooms, employee break areas, etc., all of this can be shared. Thus with less overhead per partner more profit flows to the bottom line.

Agree on values and principles. If partners agree on values and principles, then the rest of the "stuff" usually can be worked out. This is if the partners want to work it out. It is not as easy as you would think to find someone of like mindset in values and principles. When you find that person, it is many times worth it to compromise and try and work through the details.

Some people shouldn't have partners. If you are someone who must control everything and your way is the only way and/or you can't tolerate someone making a mistake, then you shouldn't have a partner. You will be happier doing what you can do and doing it your way instead of being frustrated when another partner doesn't complete the task on your timetable or doesn't do it the way you want it done. The beauty of a partnership is that you don't have to do everything, but if you spend more time redoing or being upset that it isn't done the "right way" then you defeat the benefit of a partnership and you would be better off without it.

Communicate, communicate, and communicate. As in any relationship, a partnership must be developed and nourished. The more you communicate and exchange information, the more your partner is kept up-to-date and feels a part of the partnership. Weekly meetings outside of the business location are recommended. Even if you don't think that you have anything to discuss, you will find that as soon as you start sharing and talking about the activities of the week, you will discover ideas that you want to bounce off of your partner.

One of the biggest complaints that I hear from partners is that they don't know what the other partner does and one or both partners believe he or she is doing everything. In reality, each is usually doing a great deal, but they aren't telling each other. A partnership that provides your livelihood, your bread and butter, and is important in your life is important enough to invest the time and energy to make it work.

Buy/sell agreement should be in writing. A buy/sell agreement should be in writing and should be developed and signed before the business is started. If you plan for your breakup at the beginning, you have a much better chance of "making it" than if you leave the breakup to chance. The likelihood that you will agree on anything when you are already upset with one another is slim to none. *When*, not if, (very few partnerships last a lifetime), you "break up," there is a document to reference and guide you through this process. My first partner and I signed our buy/sell agreement before we started our partnership and I was so thankful that we did. We were married to brothers and when I filed for divorce from my husband it became difficult for us to remain in business together. We were able to refer to our agreement and the procedure for my buying her out and it prevented adding more friction to the already strained family situation. Otherwise we may have ended up in court where a Judge would have had to split up our partnership. This would have been expensive and the Judge may have dictated a conclusion that neither one of us liked.

Partners don't want to be in business with someone else. When you go into partnership with someone, you make that decision based on the personality and the information that you have currently. Very few partners are willing to be in business with one person one day and then without notice or being able to vote, are in business with a different person or persons the next day. One way to prevent this is to provide within the buy/sell agreement the procedure for a partner to leave the partnership. Forrest didn't want to be in business with Charles' children, but he didn't have a choice.

The death of a partner. The death of a partner is usually an involuntary withdrawal of participation in a partnership. But it does not terminate their partnership interest or the value of their partnership interest. Unless there is a procedure and a way to fund the buying of the deceased partner's interest from the family, the remaining partner will be in business with a spouse and/or children of the deceased partner. It is important to state in the buy/sell agreement that upon the death of one partner, their interest should be offered for purchase by the remaining partner by a particular date. The issues that must be provided for are the valuation of the interest and the terms for purchase.

Valuation of partnership interest in case of death. Value is normally determined by a willing buyer and a willing seller. In the case of a limited market, such as a small partnership, this independent buyer and seller concept is not available and valuation becomes a little harder. I don't recommend that you select a valuation clause which states, "the value shall be determined annually by the partnership." The partners expect to get together each year and decide the annual valuation, but they don't meet, or they don't come to an agreement on the value. Then a partner dies and there is no stated valuation. This type of clause should be avoided because it doesn't work.

I also don't recommend the clause, "the value is to be determined by the firm's CPA or another CPA agreed to by the partners." There are so many variables in valuing a small business that it is difficult to find a CPA who is versed in valuation methods and who has the expertise to do this. I recommend a formula be determined that considers the industry of the business and that the partners can agree best values the partnership. It may be something like: "one times average gross revenue for the last three years plus the fair market value of equipment, account receivable and inventory less liabilities." As long as the partners agree and it is reasonable for the industry, it should be included in the agreement.

Valuation in the case of a partner wanting to leave a partnership and stay locally to compete. You don't want to encourage a partner to ask to leave a partnership when there are disagreements between the partners. The departing partner could potentially become competition to the original business. If leaving is too easy a process the partner may not want to work through issues but just jump ship when the going gets tough. Many times in this kind of situation the business is valued at the book value of the assets of the partnership and no value for goodwill is computed. Again the provisions for this kind of dissolution need to be included in the buy/sell agreement.

Paying a partner the value of their partnership interest can be in a lump sum or in installment payments. In planning for the death of a partner, purchasing life insurance for the value of the partnership interest on each partner is recommended. This provides for cash to buy out the partner's family as soon as possible and reduce the cash required out of the business to purchase the deceased partner's interest. Each partner owns life insurance on each other's life and the life insurance proceeds are restricted to purchase the other partner's partnership interest upon death.

I have seen a trust utilized when there are more than two partners to prevent a large number of life insurance policies from being purchased. One life insurance policy is purchased on each partner's life and the proceeds are distributed to the remaining partners to purchase the partnership interest from the deceased partner's family. Unfortunately, there isn't insurance that you can purchase that is called "partner wants to leave insurance." So when a partner wants to leave a partnership, the funding must come from the partnership assets, other assets from the remaining partner or partners, or borrowed money from a bank.

Borrowing money from a bank may be difficult unless there are enough partnership assets or partner assets to use as collateral. As a practical matter you don't want to hand a partner a lump sum to compete against you anyway. In these cases you may want to establish procedures to pay for the re-purchase of the partnership interest over a period of time or with an installment agreement. Installment payments over three to ten years, depending on the value of the partnership, may be appropriate. You don't want the payments to cripple the business or restrict too much of the growth of the business.

Order of offering to buy out partner. Some buy/sell agreements with more than two partners have a procedure for requesting the buy out. Many times the buy out is first offered to the partnership and the partnership usually has a period of thirty days to accept or decline. If the offer is declined, than it is offered to the individual partners with thirty more days to decline. If the partners decline, then the partner who wants to be bought out is free to go to the open market to try and sell their interest. There is usually a limited market for a partial interest in a small business. As a practical basis, most partners don't want to be in business with strangers and either the partnership or one or more of the partners will try and exercise the buy out provisions outlined in the buy/sell agreement. If the partnership buys the partnership interest, the percentage ownership of the remaining partners is preserved and most partners prefer this. If one or more partners purchase the outgoing partner's partnership interest, the percentage of ownership of the remaining partner changes and the partnership ownership may change.

Non-compete agreement. You may not want your former partner to compete against the partnership. A non-compete agreement for a particular geographical area and for existing customers (for one to five year period) should be included in the buy/sell agreement. Some states make it difficult to enforce non-compete agreements. If you can't enforce a pure non-compete, as it prevents someone from making a living in your state, you can include a formula for them to compensate the partnership for taking clients or customers from the partnership. An example is that the withdrawing partner will pay the partnership 20% of revenue generated for the next five years from existing clients or customers of the partnership. Again, by having this in writing before there is a disagreement, the partnership will be protected.

Remember that being right doesn't mean it doesn't cost you money. Even though you have a buy/sell agreement and it is signed and executed, one or more of the partners can contest it. It doesn't mean that they will prevail, but they can sue and try to have a Judge throw out the buy/sell agreement. The partner who sues the other partner usually wants the Judge to decide something in their favor. I recommend that you have separate attorneys advise each partner during the negotiation process of the buy/sell agreement and have an attorney for the partnership. It may seem that you are paying extra in attorney fees but paying them up front may negate them on the back end.

Anyone can sue for any reason. Being right doesn't mean it doesn't cost you money to defend your position and win in court. When partners get angry with one another sometimes reason goes out the window and attorneys are the only ones who win in these situations. If there is a buy/sell agreement in place and a partner takes it to an attorney, it may reduce the likelihood of a suit. The attorney may explain to the partner that he or she would likely be told to comply with the agreement in court.

Consider avoiding 50/50 partnerships. With 50/50 partnerships no one partner has the final decision. If there is a disagreement there is no one to break the tie. I have seen great partnerships with 50/50 ownership but these have been few and far between. The more successful partnerships have one person owning 51% or more and this partner can make the final decision. The ownership and compensation can be different percentages. You can have different ownership percentages and share compensation equally and treat most decisions as if you are equal partners. The majority owner can exercise their ability to have the final decision only when there are unresolved decisions.

When a 50/50 partnership works. Sometimes you find a partner and a 50/50 split of everything works. Both partners put their egos aside and work toward decisions that are best for the partnership as a whole, and not necessarily decisions that are best for them individually. I have found a few of these partnerships among my clients and they have worked because each partner tried to make it work. They divided the responsibilities and trusted each other to get the job done and to involve the other partner when necessary. They made a special effort to communicate and keep each other up to date. When disagreements occurred they sat down either agreed to disagree or compromised for the good of the partnership. They still had buy/sell agreements for ultimate termination, but they worked at making the partnership successful.

The most important thing in partnerships, limited liability companies, corporations, etc., with more than one owner is to have a buy/sell agreement in writing at the beginning of the business. This allows for the partners to relax and work on the business and the partnership and when a breakup happens they don't have to spend time, energy and money figuring out what to do. If Charles and Forrest had taken the time to establish a buy/sell agreement and a partnership and operating agreement, they would have functioned much more efficiently.

BUSINESS PLANS & BUDGETS CHECKLIST

	Strategy	Page Ref #	Application To Your Business
1.	Partner vs Owner vs Shareholder	33	
2.	Something must be gained by each partner for them to stay together	34	
3.	Misunderstandings occur when details are not discussed ahead of time	34	
4.	It is a trade off: having a partner or being in business by yourself	34	
5.	Partners may not do it exactly the way that you would	34	
6.	The things that make you successful are the very things that can drive you crazy	34	
7.	Respect and accept your partner's differences	35	
8.	Sometimes a third party mediator can help	35	
9.	Outside board members or an advisory board	35	
10.	Agree to disagree	35	
11.	Be yourself	36	

	Strategy	Page Ref #	Application To Your Business
12.	More ideas	36	
13.	Built-in sounding board	36	
14.	Divide and conquer tasks	36	
15.	Partnership and operating agreement	37	
16.	Don't compete with your partner	37	
17.	Partners can make more money with sharing overhead	37	
18.	Agree on values and principles	38	
19.	Some people shouldn't have partners	38	
20.	Communicate, communicate, and communicate	38	
21.	Buy/sell agreement should be in writing	38	
22.	Partners don't want to be in business with someone else	39	
23.	The death of a partner	39	
24.	Valuation of partnership interest in case of death	39	

	Strategy	Page Ref #	Application To Your Business
25.	Valuation in the case of a partner wanting to leave a partnership and stay locally to compete	40	
26.	Paying a partner the value of their partnership interest can be in a lump sum or in installment payments	40	
27.	Order of offering to buy out partner	41	
28.	Non-compete agreement	41	
29.	Remember that being right doesn't mean it doesn't cost you money	42	
30.	Consider avoiding 50/50 partnerships	42	
31.	When a 50/50 partnership works	43	

CHAPTER 5
Choosing Your Professional Team

When Jennifer started her business, she wanted to do everything herself. She incorporated her business by going to the Secretary of State's website where she completed and filed basic boiler plate incorporation papers. She wanted to save money so she didn't order a corporate book with the sample minutes and corporate stock certificates. She did open a separate bank account and decided to do her accounting using hand spreadsheets. She listed in the incorporation papers that she intended for her business to be a Sub Chapter S corporation for income tax purposes. However, she failed to file the necessary election with the Internal Revenue Service. Believing that she was an S Corporation, she didn't pay herself a salary and took distributions from corporate earnings.

Jennifer didn't purchase business liability insurance or separately insure her business equipment.

She operated three years and filed Sub-Chapter S Income Tax Returns. She had a misunderstanding with one of her customers and they sued her and things began to unravel.

Jennifer hired an attorney to defend her company. After the attorney reviewed the case, she explained to her that the corporate shield could be pierced by the plaintiff because no stock certificates were ever issued or minutes ever recorded of corporate meetings. She did not have the limited liability protection that she thought she had with a corporation. She did not have insurance, so her personal assets were at risk in the lawsuit. The attorney referred her to a CPA.

After reviewing the situation, the CPA explained that without an S Election on a Form 2553 timely filed with the Internal Revenue Service she had not officially elected Sub-S status and therefore was not a Sub-Chapter S Corporation. All of the Sub-Chapter S returns would have to be corrected and amended to C-Corporate returns and taxes would have to be paid at the corporate level. She would also incur penalties and interest on the unpaid corporate taxes. Her personal returns would need to be amended. Instead of distributions, she would need to record dividends as ordinary income. The same income was being taxed twice, once at the corporate level and once at the personal level. The exposure of her personal assets to the lawsuit, the lack of appropriate insurance and the double taxation debacle were the results of failing to become properly informed and trying to do things herself. How could Jennifer have avoided her mistakes?

Consider buying knowledge. I once learned at a seminar that you can buy knowledge or you can learn through the school of hard knocks. Both are expensive, but in buying knowledge you save valuable time, money and headaches. It has been my experience that you save more money on the front end.

Seek legal advice and set up your business correctly. Jennifer should have taken time to choose a professional team to advise her from the beginning on the best way to set up her business. Most people seek an attorney to advise them on which legal entity to choose. I have an entire chapter devoted to choosing the appropriate legal entity, see Chapter 3, *Choosing Your Legal Entity*.

If Jennifer had used an attorney to incorporate, the attorney would have included in his or her price the corporate book with the stock certificates and the minute book. The attorney would have instructed Jennifer to issue the stock certificate in her name and put it in a safe place such as a safe deposit box. He or she would have also prepared her initial organizational meeting minutes. Many times the annual meetings are held at the attorney's office and the attorney prepares the annual meeting minutes for the corporate book.

By establishing a relationship with an attorney up front this person is available to provide advice along the way. By having agreements clearly spelled out for each side, the attorney can prepare contracts that can be used in the business to prevent misunderstandings with customers. If you are going to form a corporation you need to respect the separate legal entity and operate as a corporation. Your attorney can assist you with this process.

Select a CPA to file the Sub-S Election and to set up the books. The attorney probably would have referred Jennifer to a certified public accountant (CPA) to discuss the Sub-S Election and to set up her books.

The CPA would have prepared the Sub-Chapter S Election for her signature and probably mailed it to the IRS and certified the return receipt to prove that it had been mailed by the due date. If Jennifer had sought the advice of a CPA she would have had her Sub-Chapter S Election filed properly.

The CPA will recommend accounting software. The CPA would also have recommended an accounting software program to Jennifer and would have provided training on the software. He or she would also have prepared the opening journal entry to start the books.

The CPA can provide tax and accounting services. CPA's can provide monthly accounting services and year end accounting and tax services. Understanding the tax laws allows CPA's to make suggestions to you before year end to save taxes. Saving taxes allows you to keep more of what you make.

Establishing a relationship with a CPA insures that this person is available to assist with obtaining all of the necessary company account numbers with the various government entities. This includes a Federal Identification Number (FIN) (sometimes referred to as the Employer Identification Number (EIN). Other account numbers that your business may be required to obtain include: a sales tax number, an alcohol tax number and tobacco tax number and other state reporting numbers.

A CPA can explain when the various returns are due and how to prepare them. If you don't want to learn how to prepare them the CPA firm can usually do this for you each month. You will know that they are prepared correctly and on time and you will have less hassle with the taxing authorities.

Employers must understand their responsibility to withhold and pay payroll taxes. Having employees requires the withholding of federal payroll taxes and the payment of these taxes. Employers are required to withhold Social Security and Medicare taxes and to match these taxes as an employer cost and remit them with the federal income taxes. The EIN is used to remit these taxes. Most states also have personal income taxes and these must be withheld as well. The CPA can assist you in applying for this state account number and tell you when these taxes are due.

There are federal unemployment taxes and most states have unemployment taxes that must be paid by the employer and are not withheld from the employee's check. This is the sole expense of the employer. Each state has wage limits for these taxes that may be different from the federal wage limit. Some payroll taxes are due to be paid to the IRS within 3 days, on a monthly basis, on a quarterly basis, or on an annual basis. Tax returns for these taxes are also due monthly, quarterly and annually.

I have explained all of these payroll taxes to illustrate that to learn about all of these taxes by yourself is time consuming and difficult to do. If you miss paying these taxes or filing any one of these returns it will generally be costly for you. It is often better to pay someone to teach you or to hire them to prepare them for you. Many times your CPA can provide these services. Sometimes, the CPA can print and deliver your checks in addition to computing the taxes due and preparing the tax returns. This is one service that is reasonable to outsource and it relieves your office staff from having to learn to prepare taxes. This frees the staff to concentrate on making more money for the firm. If your CPA does not provide these services you can contact a payroll service.

Select an insurance professional. Both Jennifer's attorney and her CPA would have referred her to an insurance professional who would have suggested that she have a number of types of insurance to protect her company, herself, her employees and to insure the company assets. Regardless of the limited liability status, there is no reason to expose any entity to undue risks. Jennifer needed to consider product liability insurance, general liability insurance, and insurance to protect the company assets.

If she had employees then workman's compensation insurance should have been obtained as well. She should also have considered providing group health and life insurance benefits for her employees. These basic benefits are important to attract qualified employees. The company is very dependent on Jennifer's ability to continue to provide services to the company and if she is unable to work or dies then the company would need to hire someone with her skills to provide these services. She needs to purchases key person disability and life insurance to provide funds in these situations.

An insurance professional would have identified Jennifer's exposure to loss and provided quotes on the various insurance policies she should consider. This person would review annually the existing policies and the status of the business and suggest revisions to the policies for the next year. If prices were increased by the current carriers then this person would shop around and provide alternative carriers and/or options to Jennifer.

Select a banker. Any one of the professionals listed above could have referred Jennifer to a friendly banker who specialized in small businesses. The banker could recommend a checking account which charged little or no service fees for small businesses. I would have recommended setting up a credit line for the business, even if Jennifer didn't think she would need it. You never know when an opportunity might appear which would require capital or when waiting on receivables to be collected might cause short term cash short falls.

Consider adopting a profit sharing or retirement plan. As your business grows you should consider a profit sharing or retirement plan for the business.

There are a number of different kinds of plans. Some plans require your employees to contribute and you as the employer can match some of the contributions. There are other plans in which you as the employer contribute solely and still others that are combinations of both types. See Chapter 18, *Retirement Plans and Other Employee Benefits*, for more detailed information on retirement plans. Your CPA can recommend a plan for your company from a tax prospective that matches your business and employee mix.

Select an investment advisor for you and the profit sharing and retirement plan. You will need an investment advisor to invest your money and the money for the employees in the profit sharing or retirement plan. Your CPA should be able to make that referral to you as well.

As your business grows and you want to increase your saving program for your retirement outside of your company retirement plan, the investment advisor can assist you with recommendations consistent with your time horizon and risk tolerance.

Your investment advisor should be able to offer you a number of different investment options with the profit sharing or retirement plan. This person should offer to have an employee meeting and explain the benefits and investment options to the employees. This person should not be a stranger to the firm and should offer to be available to the employees for consultation on a regular basis. As the company grows and the employee mix changes, you should receive recommendations from both your CPA and your financial advisor as to recommended changes in your profit sharing or retirement plan. See Chapter 18 for more on retirement plans.

What characteristics should you look for in each of these professionals?

As you interview and choose your professional team (an attorney, a CPA, insurance professional, a banker and a financial advisor) you should feel comfortable with every member. You should respect them and they should have the credentials that are required for their profession.

You should ask for references and verify their licenses. With the Internet you can research state websites to verify that your professionals have current licenses. You should be able to call them and receive a timely response and feel comfortable sharing your personal and financial issues with them. They should be proactive and offer solutions to your challenges.

They should all work as a team and not as independent advisors by respecting one another. The advantage of obtaining referrals from each professional is that if you connect with one of them and they connect with the advisor that they refer to you, chances are you will connect with the referral.

You can certainly use the yellow pages and interview a number of advisors. This normally takes a significant amount of time and may cost money to meet with each one. Most business owners don't have the time to do this. Referrals are usually the fastest and best way to obtain advisors.

Another way to choose a professional is to attend a seminar about a topic that affects your business and where one of these professionals is making the presentation. This allows you see them in action. You can learn more about their knowledge in your industry and see if you connect with them.

If Jennifer had taken time and decided that having professionals to advise her business was important, she would not have made such crucial mistakes. She would not have failed to issue stock certificates, failed to prepare annual minutes of corporate meetings and failed to file the Sub-Chapter S Election. It would have saved her time, money and headaches. I encourage you to invest the time to select your professional team to work with you. Pick a team to help you design, manage, modify, and eventually sell your business.

Taking the time to select a group of experts to provide you and your business with professional advice will allow you to use more of your valuable time to do the things at which you are an expert. The right team of experts can help keep you out of trouble, help you plan for the future, and help you be more successful in your business.

CHOOSING YOUR PROFESSIONAL TEAM CHECKLIST

	Strategy	Page Ref #	Application To Your Business
1.	Consider buying knowledge	48	
2.	Seek legal advice and set up your business correctly	48	
3.	Select a CPA to file the Sub S Election and to set up the books	49	
4.	The CPA will recommend accounting software	49	
5.	The CPA can provide tax and accounting services	49	
6.	Employers must understand their responsibility to withhold and pay payroll taxes	50	
7.	Select an insurance professional	51	
8.	Select a banker	51	
9.	Consider adopting a profit sharing or retirement plan	51	
10.	Select an investment advisor for you & the profit sharing and retirement plan	52	
11.	What characteristics should you look for in each of these professionals	52	

CHAPTER 6
Choosing Your Business Location & Negotiating Your Lease

Larry decided to open his new company in an industrial office park. He owns a camera store where he sells cameras and develops pictures for customers. There is a median in the road and customers have to go past his store and do a u-turn to come back to his store. There are a number of mature trees in the parking lot and visibility of his sign from the street is limited. He is four miles from any retail stores and strip plazas. He wants to move his business but his lease doesn't allow him to sub-lease and he has two years left on the contract. His sales are slow and below his projections and he may have to close his business. Larry needs help.

Location, Location, Location. How many times have we heard that in relation to our personal residences? This also applies to businesses.

Make it easy for your customers to find you. Larry needs to determine where his customers are located and where they are most likely to look for him. He then needs to make it easy for them to find him. If he wants customers to discover him by walking by his store, (this is called walk in traffic) he needs to consider locating in a retail center with stores and restaurants that attract people who are likely to be his customers. He needs to determine the demographics of the customers and where are they likely to shop?

Make it easy for your customers to do business with you. Customers may want to drop off their pictures and shop and then stop by on their way home and pick up their completed pictures. If the store were located in or near a shopping area this would make it easy for the customers to do business with Larry.

Visibility from the street. Visibility is so important for a retail business. Customers get frustrated if they are looking for you and can't find you. They will go to the competition if they are easier to find than you are. If Larry has to remain for the duration of his lease, he needs to negotiate with his landlord to have the trees trimmed and put signs near the street to point people to his store. In a new location, Larry needs to consider where his sign will be located and make sure that it can be seen from all angles on the street.

Easy access. At Larry's current location, customers have to make a u-turn and double back to his store. This is dangerous in the best of circumstances and some customers may not be willing to do this on a regular basis—especially if it is easy to get in and out of the parking lot of the competition.

Niche market. When you have a store location that is not near your customers, you need to work extra hard and spend marketing dollars to bring the customers to you. You also have to make it worth their while to come see you once they get there. Some businesses can do this if they have a niche market or they are experts in a particular field and the customers don't have choices. My family needed to have the color of their oven doors changed and this required a company that could put a special heat resistance color on them. There were only a couple of places in Atlanta that did this work. We were willing to go to go wherever to get this done because it was cheaper than buying new ovens. Since this required specialized equipment and expertise few businesses offered this service. The businesses which did the work catered to a niche market, therefore location was not as much of an issue for them.

Unique business. Larry's camera store isn't as specialized and there are many options for customers in any given city to get their pictures developed and buy camera equipment. So Larry needs to offer something else to set himself apart. Service, price, and turn-around time on pictures are just a few of the things he needs to consider to differentiate his business in his customer's minds. This also makes location even more important to Larry's business. Customers may not be willing to go out of their way to find Larry if they can find what they want at another competitor's who is more in sync with their normal shopping patterns.

Renegotiate. If Larry decides that he really needs to move then he needs to sit down with his landlord and see if he or she will work with him. He should explain to the landlord that if he remains in the lease his business and he won't have the money to pay anyway. If Larry offers to advertise and find another tenant for the landlord under the same terms, maybe the landlord would release him from the lease.

The landlord's main concern is having a paying tenant. Since sub-leasing is not an option, doing the work for the landlord to secure another tenant may solve the problem. If Larry can't find someone who will pay the full amount then he can go back to the landlord and see if there is any room to negotiate a sub-leasing situation where Larry makes up the difference. Remember things in the business world often change. Although the landlord is not required to renegotiate he or she may also understand that Larry could default on the lease. Default could mean a court battle and the landlord won't get anything if Larry is bankrupt.

As Larry looks for a new location he needs to consider among other things: visibility from the street, accessibility, and customer location.

Adequate storage. Larry also needs adequate storage for his inventory and an area in the back of the store to unload and unpack new inventory. If he repairs cameras he needs a place to do this and to store the cameras awaiting repair and/or pickup. Having adequate storage for seasonal promotions and accounting records is also important.

Adequate parking. In planning for your own business remember that once your customers find you they need to be able to park close to your business. This is especially important when the weather is unpleasant. Visit the parking lot of place you are considering several times during the day. Make sure you go during lunchtime, after work, and around the dinner hours. Make sure that the parking lot doesn't fill up with the customers of the tenants who are already there. When building permits are pulled for construction there are usually rules regarding the number of parking spaces per square foot. However, the permits my not consider the number of spaces taken by employees or that customers often come one per vehicle.

Designated special parking spaces. In retail locations parking up close to a store can be hard to find—especially at peak times of the day. If there are a number of restaurants in the building then the lunch and the dinnertime patrons may take all of the prime parking spots. If Larry's customers just want to run in and pick up their pictures or their repaired camera, they may become frustrated. Larry should consider including in his lease one or two parking spots right in front for his store only. He may want to have all of the number of spaces that he is guaranteed in the lease marked on the pavement or have upright signs installed. He needs to determine with the landlord which one of them will pay for this marking.

Expansion. Larry needs to consider the options for expansion at the new location. As his business grows will he need more space and will he have to move again, or can he build in expansion options? Finding a location which has a business that has a shorter lease next door and requesting first right of refusal on that space may allow for expansion in the same location. This is important if there are choices of spaces in the complex. If there is a vacant space next to the one that Larry is considering, he could pay for an option for that space in one or two years, so that he could use this space for expansion. He needs to weigh the cost of the option with the cost of moving and re-training customers and the possible loss of customers with the move.

Near transportation hubs. Many businesses need to be near transportation hubs to take their goods to market or to receive items for resale. If you want to reduce the cost of freight, the cost of production, or replenish product for distribution faster, select a space that is close to an airport, bus or train depot, and that can transport your product.

Warehouse and distribution. Some businesses require warehouse space and office space. Some industrial office parks will have office space in the front of the space and warehouse space in the back with loading docks for freight trucks. This allows the office space to be at the same location as the warehouse space and allows office employees to monitor warehouse activities. These locations allow products to be stored and distributed on demand to store locations.

Image. Sometimes image is important in selecting a space. It needs to reflect success but not be so expensive that your customers assume that you don't need their business or that your fees/prices will be exorbitant to pay for the office space. Be tasteful and yet practical. A lot can be done with colors and accents to warm up an office space without paying extra rent per square foot.

Have an attorney review lease. Most landlords or property managers hand you a lease and explain that this is the lease and that it is the standard lease that everyone needs to sign. They will tell you that they don't make changes but every lease is subject to negotiation. The landlord's lease is written to protect the landlord; it may or may not have many clauses to protect the tenant. Protecting the tenant is not the landlord's concern. You should always have your attorney look at the lease before you sign it. Your attorney is looking out for you and will offer suggestions for changes to the lease to protect you.

Options to renew. Options to renew your lease at a specified rate are important. If you like the location then you can stay longer. If you don't like it or find a better one you can move on.

Tenant improvements. Most locations require modifications to the inside space to accommodate the business that is located there. The landlord can pay for these improvements and include it in the rental rate or the tenant can pay for them and pay less rent.

The advantage to having the landlord pay for the tenant improvements is that the tenant doesn't have to use their own money or credit resources before the doors are open to fund these improvements and the tenant can spread the cost of these improvements over the lease period by having it included in the rent payments.

If you as the tenant have to pay for these improvements it is hard to find credit resources to loan you the money to improve someone else's building. There really isn't any collateral to offer when someone else owns the property.

Many times the lease will allow for 'x' dollars per square foot of improvements to be paid by the landlord and the extra to paid by the tenant. Again this is subject to negotiation. It is important to have the space plans drawn up by the landlord's space planner or architect before the lease is signed to determine the costs of the improvements. Before the lease is signed make sure that what you want to do with the space is possible.

Many times after the plans are drawn the landlord may realize that you are the type of tenant that he or she wants in his building and be more willing to negotiate. Either way, you will want to know up front what you need to negotiate in the lease and what you may have to pay for yourself.

Measure the space. Don't assume that the space listed in the lease is correct. Measure it. I actually measured a space that I was considering renting one time and it was incorrect and the landlord claimed that his secretary had put the wrong number in the lease. If I had signed it, I would have paid a higher rent that I should have for the space. Don't assume everything is correct.

How much space do you really need? Be realistic about the space that you need. Prepare a list of the functions that you need to be covered. Can some functions be covered in the same space? Visit the competition and see how they do it. Improve upon it if you can. Don't have things so tight that your customers feel cramped and uncomfortable in your store. Make sure that someone can monitor the customer's activities in the store and notice when they need service to prevent shop lifting. Therefore, shelves should not be too high in the store so more floor space may be needed to display the same amount of inventory. Consider having the entrance door next to the cashier location so that customers coming and going can be monitored. Be careful not to take on too much overhead too soon. Some expansion room is important but too much too soon can be very expensive and limit your options in the future.

Common area costs. If you are in a building that has other tenants, the costs of the common areas is usually shared by all of the tenants based on square footage. Make sure the services that the landlord will provide are outlined in the lease. I was once in a small building with two other tenants and the entrance area had a chandelier that hung from the second story ceiling and on the outside of the building there were a number of light fixtures. There was no provision in the lease for who was going to pay for and change the light bulbs. I just assumed that the landlord would pay for this since all three of us were in the building. He did not replace them. The outside fixtures were accessible with a step ladder but the chandelier required a ladder that would extend to the second story. The other two tenants didn't care whether it was lit or not. I frequently saw clients in the evening and having light in the entry way was important. I had to pay for someone to come and replace the light bulbs and I had no recourse against the landlord or the other tenants. Make sure that these items are addressed whether it is a small or large building.

Air conditioning and heating. Check to see if you will have a thermostat in your space and whether you are able to separately control not only the temperature but the on/off switch as well. Large buildings may have central units and have standard hours that the air conditioning or heat units are running. If you want them turned on at other times you have to pay an hourly amount and set it up several days in advance. This may limit utilization of the space at the last minute to meet with a customer or client during off hours. Make sure that you have a thermostat in your office suite. I worked at a firm one time that didn't have a thermostat in their office. The office had been split off from another office that had downsized and sub-leased the space to us. The thermostat was in their location so we were at their mercy for our temperature.

Real estate taxes, building insurance and common area costs. The base rent is usually set with that year's real estate, building insurance, and common costs known. In future years these costs may go up and the landlord will want to pass the increase on to the tenant. The real estate assessments are determined by the government and many times these are passed down within a designated number of days of the landlord being notified of the increase and then the tenant has a specified number of days to pay the increase as additional rent. Make sure that these guidelines are outlined and that the landlord can't just show up at your business and expect you to write a check.

The rest of the costs should be tied to a published rate of inflation or a specified maximum increase each year. Find out the governing body which oversees the common areas and the procedure for notifying them of problems. Determine what rights you have and how you get a procedure or rule changed.

Security systems. There are some important questions you must ask concerning the security system. What kind of security systems are included in the lease? Are there security officers who patrol the parking lots and check the outside doors of the building at night? Is there a security officer at the entrance and are the customers and tenants required to sign in and out after hours? Are you allowed to put your own security system in your space? Decide which features are important to you, your customers and your business and negotiate this into the lease.

Personal guarantee. If the assets in your business are not sufficient to provide collateral for the lease or they are pledged for other loans, the landlord may require a personal guarantee from the tenant-owners?). Try and negotiate so that you don't have to do this. Or at least request that after a year or so of making the payments that you are released from the guarantee. This could limit your personal borrowing ability. In some cases the landlord will not negotiate and the personal guarantee is required for the lease period. If it is required, request the option to substitute another personal guarantee with the same or better net worth and be released from the guarantee. This would be important if you sell the business and you want the new buyer to provide the personal guarantee after the sale instead of you.

Right to assign to another entity. It is also important to include in your agreement the right to assign the lease to another entity. It is important to give you flexibility if you change legal entities. For example you could incorporate a sole proprietorship or take on a partner or form a partnership or limited liability company. You could sell the business and want to assign the lease to the buyer. The landlord may want the right to approve the new assignee. If the business activity has not substantially changed the approval should not be necessary or required by the landlord.

Ability to Sublease. The ability to sublease is very important to accommodate flexibility and changes in your business. It is important for you to be able to find another tenant to take over your lease. This allows you to move your business without having to pay for two locations. The landlord may want the ability to approve the tenant. This is acceptable within reason. If the landlord is going to consider releasing you from the lease then the approval process is appropriate. If you are still on the hook for the lease if the sub-lease tenant defaults, then the approval by the landlord needs to be with grounds. The landlord shouldn't be able to disapprove just because he or she doesn't like the way the tenant looks or talks. Your attorney can offer the appropriate language to protect you.

Lease needs to protect both the landlord and the tenant. The lease needs to protect both the landlord and the tenant. It needs to be fair and outlined in writing and contain as many provisions for "what could happen" as possible. This is so that the relationship between you and the landlord is not strained. The lease becomes a working tool to govern that relationship. Most landlords just want to be paid and most tenants just want to make a living in their business. The lease helps each of you do this.

Virtual office. Non retail operations don't necessarily need a storefront location. Many small businesses prefer to go to their customers or can work from a home office. Having a virtual office location works best for them to keep their overhead down. Customers have a business location to drop off or pick up packages, and these services many times provide for the answering of the business phone lines and voice mail services. Some virtual office packages will transfer calls to your cell phone so that you don't have to be anywhere near the office. This allows it to appear that you are in the office for the customer's call. You can use this location for your mailing address and receive your mail there. These services can include access to conference rooms or day offices upon reservation. These amenities can either be included in the monthly package or offered at an hourly fee. Then if you need to meet with a customer at your business location you can still appear professional.

Mail location only. If you don't need to have your phone answered or meet clients in a conference room but want to have the ability to receive mail and other packages away from your home office, there are companies that offer this service as well. UPS Stores, Office Supply stores and others are often located in a strip plaza and can offer mail services, etc.

There are many things to consider when choosing your business location and negotiating your lease. I encourage you to take into consideration all of the points which have been made to prevent your business from suffering the consequences of acting too quickly or without proper information. The location of your business can be the key to the success or failure of your business.

CHOOSING YOUR BUSINESS LOCATION & NEGOTIATING YOUR LEASE CHECKLIST

	Strategy	Page Ref #	Application To Your Business
1.	Location, Location, Location	55	
2.	Make it easy for your customers to find you	55	
3.	Make it easy for your customers to do business with you	56	
4.	Visibility from the street	56	
5.	Easy access	56	
6.	Niche market	56	
7.	Unique business	56	
8.	Renegotiate	57	
9.	Adequate storage	57	
10.	Adequate parking	57	
11.	Designated special parking spaces	58	
12.	Expansion	58	
13.	Near transportation hubs	58	
14.	Warehouse and distribution	58	

	Strategy	Page Ref #	Application To Your Business
15.	Image	59	
16.	Have an attorney review lease	59	
17.	Options to renew	59	
18.	Tenant improvements	59	
19.	Measure the space	60	
20.	How much space do you really need?	60	
21.	Common area costs	60	
22.	Air conditioning and heating	61	
23.	Real estate taxes, building insurance and common area costs	61	
24.	Security systems	61	
25.	Personal guarantee	62	
26.	Right to assign to another entity	62	
27.	Ability to Sublease	62	
28.	Lease needs to protect both the landlord and the tenant	63	
29.	Virtual office	63	
30.	Mail location only	63	

CHAPTER 7
Raising Capital

Matthew has prepared a business plan. He wanted to start his business with his own money and resources and has found he doesn't have enough. Matthew now wants to explore other options of raising capital.

Undercapitalization of new businesses is a major reason that new businesses fail. A lack of capital or an underestimation of how much is "enough" capital is a major reason that new businesses fail. Preparing a realistic business plan which accurately forecasts future capital needs is very important. It can be hard to find sources of capital when the company hasn't starting making money yet. This can be true for a start-up company or for a company that has been in existence for a while but isn't yet profitable.

Business plan is a requirement. A complete business plan including financial projections must be prepared to recruit capital for the business. Assumptions need to be outlined and described for the reader to evaluate. The business plan will determine how much capital is required to start the business. This business plan should include the initial assets that need to be purchased by the company to start it and the anticipated working capital that will be required to operate the company for the first three to five years. It is also important to include compensation for the owner/employee of the company in the projections. For more information on how to prepare a business plan, see Chapter 2, *Business Plans and Budgets*.

Equity versus debt. Debt has to be repaid, equity does not. Upon liquidation of assets, creditors are paid before equity owners. The equity owners then receive their proportionate interest of the remaining liquidated assets. The equity owners could receive less than their original investment or more than their original investment. This depends upon the amount of debt.

Friends and family may be able to assist you. Friends and family may be willing to gift you money to start your new business. Gifts do not have to be repaid and are preferable to loans. Alternatively, friends and family may want to become equity owners in your new company. I recommend retaining majority ownership. See Chapter 4, *Partnerships and Buy/Sell Agreements*, for a full explanation of the pros and cons of retaining majority ownership and information on how to structure this kind of agreement properly. Often, however, friends and family will prefer to loan you money for your new business. Many times, they are willing to accept the risk of loaning you money because they believe in you and they are willing to accept a higher level of risk than a third party lender would be. However these types of loans have the potential to cause significant conflicts within a family. Other siblings or family members may find out about it and become jealous or otherwise create tension at family gatherings.

If the business is successful and you repay the loan according to plan, then everyone will be happy. If you default on the loan or are not able to pay the loan payments, or if you lose the money altogether, there may be repercussions within your family. Losing your business and your family at the same time is a worst-case scenario. Thus, since there are so many unknowns in the development and growth of your business, I caution you about using family members as a source of raising capital.

Borrow equity in real estate. If you have equity in your personal home or rental properties, consider obtaining an equity line or mortgage on these properties to finance your business. Make sure that you can still make the payments if you business fails, otherwise, you will have to sell your home or your rental properties to pay off the loan.

Bank loans. Depending on your credit score, business experience, and the collateral available, your bank may loan you money through the collateralizing assets of your new business and your personal guarantee. This option is worth exploring as it leaves other financial options available if you need them. However, keep in mind that your personal guarantee leaves you personally liable for any default.

SBA guaranteed loans. Sometimes banks like your business plan but they are unwilling to solely accept the risk of loaning you the money. The Small Business Administration can step in and guarantee the bank loan so that if you default they pay the bank for you. These loans are usually at a lower interest rate than the bank would normally charge and longer payment options are sometimes available. With lower interest rates and longer payment options the monthly payments are usually lower than traditional financing. This can assist a new small business owner in establishing their business with lower monthly debt payments. SBA loans are also sometimes available when businesses expand their product or service lines, open new stores, or buy other businesses. This is an option that should always be considered. For this type of loan, there is extensive paperwork that must be completed and certain documents must be provided to qualify. SBA loan officers and the Small Business Development Centers (SBDC's) around the country can assist you with this paperwork. Some CPA's can offer assistance in preparing the forecasted financial statements that are required.

Grants may be available. There may be grants available:

1) For your type of business, or
2) For businesses that service a niche marketplace, or
3) For businesses in which your ownership or the majority of your ownership qualifies as a minority group.

There are companies that assist you in applying for grants. Again, your business plan is your starting point. Each grant has an application form and the committee that approves these grants usually insists that the information requested on the application be included in the appropriate space on the application form so they can compare numerous applications. Keep in mind that even though they may be extra work, grants are better than loans, as they generally do not have to be repaid.

However, they may or may not have tax consequences for the recipient. Check with your tax advisor about your situation. Even if the grant is taxable, paying the taxes at your tax rate (20 to 50% of grant) is still significantly cheaper than earning the money and paying taxes on the earnings and using the earning's net of taxes (120 to 200% of loan) to repay a loan or debt.

Venture capitalists. Venture capital firms have pools of capital, usually organized as a limited partnership. Private investors or institutions, such as banks and pension funds, invest their money in small, fast-growing companies who cannot raise funds on the stock market. They can invest in companies at any stage of the business cycle. The investors request a percentage equity interest in the company in exchange for medium or long-term financing—usually for five to seven years. They may request a board of director's position and offer business expertise to the board of directors and management.

Angel investors. An angel investor is an individual with money to invest in the early-stage or start-up phases of companies. These investors receive equity ownership. You will need to negotiate the percentage of ownership an angel investor will receive. If what you are selling or making is your idea or product or service, I would recommend retaining at least majority interest. Many angels will take a silent partnership role, provided the business goes according to plan. If the business gets into trouble, they may have provisions that allow them to take a more active role to save the company.

Angels can be someone you already know, a business associate, a customer, or a vendor. They could be someone that you were referred to by a mutual friend or someone that you found on the Internet. There are a number of websites that offer directories and opportunities to post requests for Angel Funding. Some even match Angels with requests.

Publicly traded stock. Companies may qualify to go public and sell their stock on one of the stock exchanges. There are many requirements to qualify, and you'll need to consult with a qualified advisor who can work with you to accomplish this goal. If you are planning to go public in the next three to five years, there are specific procedures that must be followed with your books, as well as various company qualifications that must be met. Further explanation is outside the scope of this book, but a business owner should certainly research the requirements of public companies thoroughly before attempting to "go public."

Other business associates or competitors. Instead of each person creating the same type of business and incurring the same basic overhead, it may make more sense for several people to team up and share expenses. This will spread the cost of the business startup among several owners, and reduce the need for outside financing. See Chapter 4, *Partnerships and Buy/Sell Agreements*, for pros and cons in this decision-making process.

Liquidate or withdraw from retirement plans. Before you decide to liquidate all or part of your qualified retirement plan, consider the tax consequences. This pot of money may be attractive, but is expensive to withdraw. You are allowed to withdraw from a plan and roll it over into a new IRA or an existing IRA within 60 days. If you keep it over 60 days, you are subject to state and federal income taxes, which range from 10% to 50%, depending on your state and your other income. If you are under 59 1/2 there is an early withdrawal penalty of 10 to 15% depending on the type of plan. So the net after taxes may only be 35 to 80% of your original amount. Some plans require 20% to be withheld for federal taxes on all distributions. This may or may not be enough to cover your federal income taxes and penalties so additional payments may be due. You would also still be liable for any state income taxes that are due and not withheld. Other plans allow you to waive the withholding, but again, you would still be liable for whatever state and federal income taxes and penalties may be due. Consult your CPA or tax advisor to compute the potential taxes before you withdraw the funds. If you use these funds, plan to set aside the taxes due and pay them according to your CPA or tax advisor's recommendation as a way of avoiding underpayment penalties.

Loans from regular 401-K plans. Be careful in obtaining a loan from your current company's 401-K plan. These loans appear to have advantages like repaying yourself with interest and not having to pay income tax on the loan. . If you leave the company to start your new business the minute you are no longer employed, your 401-K account will be frozen and your loan will immediately be considered a distribution or withdrawal.

These loans are only available to employees and you are no longer an employee. If you do not repay it before you leave the company you will be subject to federal and state income taxes and if you are under 59 1/2 you will also have to pay early withdrawal penalties. You could end up no better off than you would have been by withdrawing the money in the beginning.

Loans from Solo 401-K plans. Some investment companies offer Solo 401-K plans to owners with no employees outside the family. These plans can allow rollovers from other plans into the Solo 401-K and permit the owner/participant to borrow against his/her vested balance. If this plan is set up for the new company and the proceeds from the former employer rolled into this plan, you can borrow and not repay yourself. This will avoid the traps of borrowing from the former employer's plan prior to termination

Corporate bonds. Another option is to issue corporate bonds to those who are willing to loan the company money and who want a fixed rate of interest and/or payments. Some bonds are straight bonds or debt of the company. Some bonds have a convertible option as well. These bonds can be converted, usually at the creditor's option to equity. These bonds are attractive because in the early stages of the business the creditors are in line before equity owners in bankruptcies or liquidations. When the company starts to make money and to grow participating in the equity may prove more profitable than the fixed interest rate payments.

Establish a relationship with a banker. Whether or not you receive your initial financing through your bank establish a relationship with a banker. If you don't know anyone at the bank introduce yourself and find out the services that they have available for small businesses. When you attend business organization meetings look for bankers who are advertising for small business Clients. It may be worth changing banks to have a friendly banker. This banker should smooth the red tape and be able to override general procedures which cause you problems. For example, your banker should expedite the replacement of ATM cards that are lost or stolen, waive bank service fees, and approve short-term loans for you.

Establish a credit line as soon as possible, even if you don't think you need it. Establish a line of credit even if you don't think you will need it. Things happen and you will be glad for that line of credit if and when the unexpected happens.

Credit cards. Some companies use credit cards for short-term financing. They are easy to obtain and it seems that the more you have, the more you can get. Be careful. Before you know it, you can have a substantial amount of debt on credit cards. Some introductory offers have low or zero percent interest rates. The expiration dates on these offers need to be recorded and other offers considered in order to transfer these amounts from one credit card to another and continue to take advantage of the low or zero percent interest rates. It is imperative that the credit card payments be paid on or before the due date. This is different than the statement cut off date. Late fees may be assessed for late payments received after the due date, even if received by the statement cut off date. The credit card companies will usually raise the interest rates when payments are not received by the due dates. Again, be careful, this method of financing requires a significant amount of managing and uses precious management time that may be better spent in other ways for the company. See Chapter 14, *Managing Cash Flow*, regarding employee use of corporate and personal credit cards.

Vendors offer deferred payment programs. Some vendors offer deferred payment programs to encourage you to purchase new products or to sell overstocked items. They may offer these programs for large purchases in anticipation of seasonal sales. Ask them periodically if they are offering any specials. This will often allow extended payment terms and you can delay paying for inventory until closer to when it is sold and turned into cash flow for your business.

Leasing assets to reduce working capital required to start business. Leasing an asset may require a smaller up-front payment than purchasing the same asset. Since the leasing company retains ownership of the asset and the related tax benefits, they may offer lower monthly payments as well. However, keep in mind, that while it may seem upon initial review that leasing is better, you do end up with a liability and no asset. You have no residual value and nothing to sell at the end of the lease. As a general rule leasing should be avoided unless it is the only way to make the start up of the company work. In this context it may be appropriate to lease certain assets. See Chapter 16, *Buying Versus Leasing Assets*, for more information about the advantages and disadvantages of buying versus leasing assets to help you make an informed decision.

Shop for used assets instead of new assets. Shop and purchase used assets to use in your company instead of new assets that may cost more. This will reduce the total working capital required to start up your company.

Consider that used assets may require more maintenance or may be less reliable than new assets, and may cost you more in maintenance costs and down-time for you business. Certain non-critical assets may be more appropriate to purchase used than others.

Shop around for the best deal and negotiate for terms. Don't purchase the assets you need at the start of your company (or during the life of your company) at the first place you look. Check several places as prices and purchase terms may vary. Sometimes you can negotiate with vendors to match competitor's prices or terms. If you have an account or credit card with one vendor and their price is higher than the competitor with whom you don't have an account or credit card, bring this to the attention of the company and see if they will match the price or suggest the same type of product but from a different manufacturer. It doesn't hurt to ask.

Use the Internet for resources and education. The Internet enables you to access a vast body of knowledge. You can use it to educate yourself on ways to raise capital, including making contacts and connections. You can also shop for and/or purchase goods and services via the Internet.

Raising capital is not a one-shot deal. Raising capital is not a one-shot deal. This will be an on-going issue and may become easier with the success of the business. Growing the company entails constantly considering creative ways to obtain financing. Expansion of product lines, establishing franchises, opening new stores and increasing sales to new levels all require an infusion of working capital to reach business goals.

Accounts receivable factoring. There are many financing companies which will loan the company money based on a percentage of the projected collectible balance of the accounts receivable. All payments are usually sent to the factoring company's lock box at their bank and the loan payments are made and the difference is deposited into your company's bank account to pay other expenses. The rates are usually higher than other forms of financing. However, this may be the only way to receive money before customers pay you so that you can meet your payroll and other overhead expenses.

Inventory and floor plan financing. Large inventory ticket items such as cars, boats and furniture may be available for special inventory financing through the supplier or your bank. If the inventory can be assigned unique item numbers, the bank or supplier may consider financing a percentage of the inventory on hand at your company. Consider that month-end inventories must be recorded, usually by a person outside of the company, to verify that it is still held by the company. As units are sold the sales invoice is produced and the cost of the product that is financed is paid to the lending institution. When the company makes a purchase of a new inventory item the invoice for the purchase is presented to the bank for them to pay their portion. There are usually inventory financing limits approved by the lending institution, which will need to be managed. Inventory liquidation sales may also need to be set up if the company is approaching the loan limit. Interest payments on the loan must be made on a monthly basis regardless of the whether any inventory has been sold.

Personal loans to the company. As an owner, you may be required to loan money from your own personal resources from time to time. Encourage the managing owner, if that is not you, to keep the cash flow projections up to date and to provide you with as much notice as possible. Establish loan terms, interest rates, and repayment terms between yourself and the business before exchanging the funds.

Repayment of debt from income requires cash and doesn't reduce taxable income. As debt is repaid from the profits of the company, cash will be used to pay the principle of the debt and will not reduce taxable income. Therefore, income taxes may be due when the cash has been used to reduce debt. Make sure that you determine your company's tax liability and set this amount aside before reducing debt so that you will have the cash to pay the taxes. Making late income tax payments is expensive and should be avoided.

Raising capital is serious business. Raising capital is serious business and can make or break your business at the beginning and during the life of your business. You must plan ahead. If you have a solid idea or business, then fight for what you want. If you try hard enough you should find the resources that you need to make your business successful. Remember when you receive the answer "no" you just haven't found the "yes." You have to keep trying if you are going to find someone to say "yes."

RAISING CAPITAL CHECKLIST

	Strategy	Page Ref #	Application To Your Business
1.	Undercapitalization of new businesses is a major reason that new businesses fail	67	
2.	Business plan is a requirement	67	
3.	Equity versus debt	67	
4.	Friends and family may be able to assist you	68	
5.	Borrow equity in real estate	68	
6.	Bank loans	68	
7.	SBA guaranteed loans	69	
8.	Grants may be available	69	
9.	Venture capitalists	70	
10.	Angel investors	70	
11.	Publicly traded stock	70	
12.	Other business associates or competitors	70	
13.	Liquidate or withdraw from retirement plans	71	

	Strategy	Page Ref #	Application To Your Business
14.	Loans from regular 401-K plans	71	
15.	Loans from Solo 401-K plans	72	
16.	Corporate bonds	72	
17.	Establish a relationship with a banker	72	
18.	Establish a credit line as soon as possible, even if you don't think you'll need it	72	
19.	Credit cards	72	
20.	Vendors offer deferred payment programs	73	
21.	Leasing assets to reduce working capital required to start business	73	
22.	Shop for used assets to use instead of new assets	73	
23.	Shop around for the best deal and negotiate for terms	74	
24.	Use the Internet for resources and education	74	
25.	Raising capital is not a one-shot deal	74	

	Strategy	Page Ref #	Application To Your Business
26.	Accounts receivable factoring	74	
27.	Inventory and floor plan financing	74	
28.	Personal loans to the company	75	
29.	Repayment of debt from income requires cash and doesn't reduce taxable income	75	
30.	Raising capital is serious business	75	

CHAPTER 8
Employees

Mickey has an engineering firm with seven employees. He hired John 60 days ago and has since noticed a negative attitude and deficiencies in the skill sets John claimed to have. Mickey could spend time and money to train John but clients are starting to complain about his attitude. What should Mickey do?

Employees need to pull their weight for the company. Smaller companies don't have the luxury of working with problem employees for an extended period of time. If one employee is not pulling his or her weight this could be the difference between making a profit and losing money for the company. Therefore smaller firms have to decide quickly about whether to keep an employee or to terminate them.

Meet with the employee to discuss issues. Ideally, Mickey should sit down with John and find out what is causing his negative attitude and why he claimed to have skills that he apparently did not. John should be advised that he must improve his attitude and obtain the necessary skills for the job. A timetable should be established for the change in behavior and the acquisition of skill sets. However, if the skill sets are critical to the job performance, Mickey may not be able to wait for John to get up to speed. John should be told in writing that if he does not change his behavior and/or obtain the skills by a particular date he will be terminated. If at the end of the interview no agreement can be reached or if the employer is not satisfied that John will attempt to change his behavior and/or acquire the skills, he should be terminated on the spot. Small companies can not afford to have disgruntled employees around to disrupt the office and upset the company's clients.

Accept resignation and consider walking them to the door. If John were to resign and offer a two week notice, I would have to take into consideration his negative attitude and let him go right away. If John is uncooperative he will likely share the firm's private business with the clients out of spite. I have seen it happen over and over with my client firms. Then the client's become involved with employee issues and this should never happen.

If you decide to let someone go in your firm, don't keep them at the office any longer than to confirm the status on all projects. Pay them, thank them, wish them the best and walk them to the door. End on a positive note don't criticize or bad mouth them. Also, don't fire someone when you are angry, take time to cool down and reassess the situation. Words can not be taken back once they are said. Sometimes it is better to wait until the next morning to decide what to do about a problem employee or a situation from the previous day.

Don't be afraid to terminate someone, even if it will cause you to be short-handed. I have found that employers tend to keep employees who need to be terminated because they are afraid of being short-handed and having to work long hours. Some employers are also reluctant to interview and hire someone new. The situation is often akin to being in a bad marriage; they would rather deal with the unhappiness that they know, than the scariness of the unknown. Employees recognize when they have control over you or have the upper hand. This isn't the way that you want to run your firm. Remember, there are no mistakes, just learning experience. It is okay to admit that you have learned something new and take action to correct it. I have never had someone tell me that they were sorry that they let the problem employee go, just that they should have done it sooner.

Many small firms don't have the luxury of time to work with employees. Larger firms have the time and resources to isolate a problem employee and set up guidelines for improvement and give them plenty of time in which to come around and be productive again. They have more money to wait it out and more employees to spread the work around. Small businesses do not have this luxury.

Employees are like children. I have discovered that employees are like children. I have had discussions about being courteous to friends and relatives with my children and then the next day I have had a similar discussion with my employees about customer service and courtesy to fellow employees etc. Employees also will not follow procedures which are not enforced. If they don't follow a procedure and no one says anything about it, they quickly learn that it is unimportant because it is not enforced. Then when you discover that procedure was not followed and mistakes happened, it is difficult to correct the employee because there was no follow up from the beginning. Certainly the employee is at fault, but it is the responsibility of management to enforce the procedures and prevent undesirable results.

Higher unemployment rate may the cheaper cost. I have known employers who were afraid to fire an employee because it would increase their unemployment tax rate for awhile. The effect of bad interactions between employees and/or between employees and clients is potentially far more costly than the unemployment tax increase associated with one firing. Take care of business in a timely fashion and the rest will take of itself. Some states have a compensation limit that once it is paid to the employee allows them to qualify for unemployment benefits when they are terminated. Contact your state unemployment tax office and determine this amount and then decide whether the employee is qualified for the job and whether you want to retain them, before they are paid the state compensation limit. This will minimize unemployment claims to your account and keep your rate from increasing for this reason. Although it is unnecessary for you as an employer to be an expert on labor law and unemployment issues, it would be a good idea to check with your accountant and a labor attorney to help you understand most of the basic employment rules for your state and your size firm.

Test for the competency of the skills required for the job. How could Mickey have handled the hiring process differently and prevented hiring someone with a negative attitude and with substandard, ill-matched skills? Mickey should have spent more time in the pre-hiring process. Perhaps administering tests directed at the specific skills required as well as personality and psychological tests, Mickey would have identified the problem areas.

Consider hiring an employment agency. Many employers hire employment agencies to screen potential employees and take the time and burden of reviewing resumes and conducting interviews away from the business owner. They may also have access to employees who are not actively looking for jobs, but who may be perfect for your business. I recommend contacting several agencies to look for you, not just one, if you go this route. The agencies charge a fee and you need to weigh this fee against the cost of your time and the benefits of utilizing an outside agency.

Employee testing is one of the benefits of using such an agency. The tests that an agency can administer include, personality testing, psychological testing, and skill testing. In smaller offices, personality and psychological testing are even more important as you do not have as many options to move employees around to better match them to departments and jobs.

Understanding different personality types is very important in small offices. I did not realize the importance of personality testing until I started my first firm and made demands on employees that were unrealistic. I didn't understand why every employee that I hired didn't look at the world or the client's job the same way that I did. I would loose patience with that employee and evidently they would get frustrated and quit. When I finally took the time to understand that each personality type processes information differently, I learned more about which personality types were more successful in my industry and modified my style to assist them in being more successful. I started having happier, more productive employees.

There are no wrong personality types, just differences, and we need people around us in business who are different from ourselves. We make better business decisions when we consider all sides of a situation. If we have only people just like ourselves around us, we won't see other ways of accomplishing tasks and we may completely miss an idea that would provide an optimized solution for ourselves or our clients. The very thing that drives us crazy about different personality types in other people is the very reason that we need to have them around us.

Different personality types can be successful. Over the years, the best partnerships that I have observed in business have been the ones with opposite personality types who have learned to appreciate each other's differences and not fight them. This appreciation is not easy to obtain for most people.

Employer needs to modify behavior with employees. Usually you have to try it your way then determine that you don't want to continue to search for new employees and invest time and money in training them only to have them get frustrated and leave. It seems counter-intuitive that an employer has to modify his or her behavior when they own the firm and hire the employee. One would assume that the employee should modify their behavior to keep their job. Unfortunately, the employee is like the child and less sophisticated and if the employer wants to motivate the employee, the employer is the one who needs to change his or her behavior.

Checklists allow staff to be more successful. When I left an international accounting firm which used checklists for every job that we did, I vowed that I would never use another checklist. As I hired new employees, I found that the employees did not have the same experience and would frequently miss things that I could see needed to be done for a client. Within one year of leaving the other firm I had every checklist back in place. Checklists were a way for an inexperienced staff to tackle a new job and become proficient in addressing certain issues or procedures in the job.

Some jobs require psychological tests. Some employers require psychological tests for certain sensitive or high level jobs. They don't want to invest time and money training a new employee, only to discover that they were emotionally unstable or had other issues which would not allow them to be successful at the firm. These tests are more expensive and the costs need to be evaluated against the benefits. Please consult with a psychologist who specializes in matching individuals with these types of jobs to learn more about this process.

Background and credit checks are sometimes required. Some firms do complete background checks including criminal and credit checks. I believe that the costs associated with these checks are worth it. Small firms can not afford to hire individuals who can put the firm's assets and client's assets at risk.

Check references. Checking references may also have better determined the kind of employee that John had been at other companies. Even if an employment agency has checked the references, the employer should personally contact them as well. I would also contact former employers, even if they are not listed as references. If the company will only release employment dates, then the most important question to ask is "would you re-hire this person if you had an opening?" If the answer is no, ask "why?" If they refuse to answer, you have your answer. It has been my experience that a job candidate with inadequate or bad references and no reasonable explanations is a potentially difficult employee for the company. Do not hire this person.

Confirm degrees listed on resume. If specific education is a prerequisite for the job, confirm that the degree was in fact received by the candidate. If they lied do not hire this person.

Large firm to small firm is a major transition. Small firms that are considering hiring employees with large firm experience need to consider the transition time that former "large firm" employees will require when they are making the transition to a small firm environment. Many employees can not make the transition. They are used to having very specialized jobs. In small firms everyone does a little of everything. An employee who says when asked to do something, "that is not my job," needs to find another job.

Trying too hard doesn't work. Also if you as the employer have to keep trying to make the relationship work with the employee, it probably needs to stop and the employee needs to go. I have been guilty of this. I would try and try to make it work and then I would begin to resent the employee and then fire them after I became mad enough at them for not changing. This is not the way to do it. It is okay to make hiring mistakes, but the real mistake is keeping the employee past the point of realizing that it is not working. This is unfair to both the employer and the employee. Former employees have returned to see me and to thank me even though I terminated them because it wasn't working. They tell me how they went on to find a job better suited for them.

Train the employee. It usually takes 60 to 90 days for an employee to learn all of the unique aspects of their job with your company. Taking the time to train them is crucial. Although it takes longer on the front end, it decreases the employee's learning curve and the employee is more successful, better at the job and is happier. Most employees want to be successful and to do a good job for their employer.

It is also important to cross train employees in a small firm. If someone is sick or unexpectedly out of the office, then the office can continue to operate as normally as possible.

If you don't train entry level employees, be clear to state this in your employment ads. Do not make an exception and hire someone without the experience or education necessary for the position you are seeking to fill. If your office is not set up to train this type of employee then it is a long shot that the employee will survive the learning process.

Although internal training is important, some external training for employees is healthy and should be scheduled. This allows for external ideas and procedures to be introduced to the firm and considered for adoption. The words that are the kiss of death of any firm are: "We have always done it this way." The world is constantly changing and firms need to be receptive to new ideas and ways of doing things or they will not survive.

Map out goals and expectations with employees. Set up at a minimum reviews every six months, 30, 60 and 90 day, are preferable. Employees appreciate feedback and it is easier to modify behavior along the way instead of waiting until it has become a habit of the employee.

Document procedures and have employee manuals. The employee manuals take time to prepare, but it takes more time to deal with mistakes which could have been prevented with properly communicated procedures. Employees and clients can be lost as a result of not having these procedures documented. There are software programs that have templates and wizards that ask you questions related to your firm and which then create a customized employee manual. You do not have to reinvent the wheel. When you have a problem, turn it into a procedure and the problem is eliminated in the future. Document that procedure and communicate it to the employees. You can't expect to hold the employee accountable for something unless it is documented and communicated. Learning by making mistakes is not a fun way to learn. Be proactive with your employees and teach them before they make mistakes.

Have regular weekly staff meetings. I have mentioned communication several times in this chapter. One of the ways to communicate with employees is through staff meetings. I recommend weekly staff meetings to coordinate client jobs and update staff on activities of the firm and new procedures. These meetings should be short and sweet and to the point. Agendas are a good tool to make the most of the time.

Many firms use emails to communicate procedures and changes to employees. Please don't rely solely on this method of communication. Re-enforce the procedure at staff meetings several times as well.

I recommend that training sessions be held at a different time than the weekly staff meetings if possible. The focus of these meetings is different that the staff meetings and everyone should come into them with expecting to learn. If the company can not have two different meeting dates for staff meetings and training meetings, then combining them is preferable to not have training included.

Fair compensation, bonuses, gifts and public recognition. Reward employees for jobs well done and goals met. Give them bonuses and gifts and public recognition. Make sure that employees are paid appropriately for the job that they do. If the company is making money share it with the employees. This keeps them motivated and loyal to your firm. If Mickey adopts these ideas, he will have a more successful firm.

Employees can help you make more money. I will never forget the advice I received from a former employer. He told me that "you can only make so much money by yourself, the real key to making money is to make it through other people." So if you want to build a company and make more than you can make on your own, you need employees. Learn how to help your employees be successful and then you will be successful.

EMPLOYEES CHECKLIST

	Strategy	Page Ref #	Application To Your Business
1.	Employees need to pull their weight for the company	79	
2.	Meet with the employee to discuss issues	79	
3.	Accept resignation and consider walking them to the door	80	
4.	Don't be afraid to terminate someone, even if it will cause you to be short-handed	80	
5.	Many small firms don't have the luxury of time to work with employees	80	
6.	Employees are like children	80	
7.	Higher unemployment rate may the cheaper cost	81	
8.	Test for the competency of the skills required for the job	81	
9.	Consider hiring an employment agency	81	
10.	Understanding different personality types is very important in small offices	82	

	Strategy	Page Ref #	Application To Your Business
11.	Different personality types can be successful	82	
12.	Employer needs to modify behavior with employees	83	
13.	Checklists allow staff to be more successful	83	
14.	Some jobs require psychological tests	83	
15.	Background and credit checks are sometimes required	83	
16.	Check references	83	
17.	Confirm degrees listed on resume	84	
18.	Large firm to small firm is a major transition	84	
19.	Trying too hard doesn't work	84	
20.	Train the employee	84	
21.	Map out goals and expectations with employees	85	
22.	Document procedures and have employee manuals	85	

	Strategy	Page Ref #	Application To Your Business
23.	Have regular weekly staff meetings	85	
24.	Fair compensation, bonuses, gifts and public recognition	86	
25.	Employees can help you make more money	86	

CHAPTER 9
Technology

Marie has a staff of six and each person has a computer at their desk all tied into a network server. She has one printer in a central location for all computers to print. She has five different programs for client service and they do not talk to one another so any changes have to be entered five times. She is frustrated as her office is not very efficient and employee productivity is lower than her industry averages.

Time is money. Every time Marie's employees' get up and go retrieve a document from the printer they waste time. Each person should have a printer in their own office. Every time the employee gets up and walks around the office they can become distracted and side-tracked. The more that Marie can keep her employees in their seats the more work they will do. Printers are relatively inexpensive compared to the loss of employee efficiency and they should be purchased as soon as possible. Marie should still keep a network printer in case one of the individual printers is broken or out of toner so there is no interruption of work.

Focus on the benefit to the firm. Sometimes employers try to save money on technology and short change their bottom line. You shouldn't focus on the cost, but focus on the benefit to the firm. If it will save your employees time, it will increase the capacity of the firm and the ability to make more money. You will also have happier, less frustrated, employees. If you are not sure of ways to improve the efficiency of your firm ask your employees. They will tell you. They live it every day.

Use integrated programs. Marie also has programs which are not integrated — the programs don't talk with one another. She should look to see if the programs can be integrated. If not, she should review the functions of the various software programs and research to see if there are other programs that will serve the same functions and that are interactive. The time saved by not having to re-enter the same data in multiple programs and the elimination of errors in re-keying the data will be significant and will help keep clients happy with the correct data. As a client, nothing is more frustrating than to know that you have given the change of address information to the firm three times it still hasn't changed in the latest communication from them.

Make a list of what you want the programs to do. Before Marie purchased her computer hardware and software she should have made a list of what she wanted the programs to do, what she did not need the programs to do, and what procedures were most important in saving time in the office. Now she should strive to automate every procedure which could save employees time in the office. Search for software that would accomplish the tasks on the list and then select programs that will integrate with each other. After determining the best software for each program required by the firm, she should then determine the hardware requirements for each program including the size and memory required.

Consult with your ITC. In your own business it is important to consult with your Information Technology Consultant (ITC) at the beginning and along the way, this will prevent you from re-inventing the wheel. Many times they can shortcut your research time, as well as tell you things that really won't work, even though the software company advertises that it will.

Budget for training. Once you have the software installed for your firm, don't stop there. The purchase price of software is only the beginning. You should put in your budget training costs as well. There is no point in having the software in your office if no one knows how to use it. Don't expect employees to learn software on their own time, they won't. Sometimes employees can learn if you allocate time in the office for them to use tutorials and training CDs. It has been my experience that unless you specify the specific items that you want them to learn they will not spend the time trying to figure things out.

Involve the employees in the training. If you don't have time to spend several days at one time learning all the things that a new software program will do teach the basics. Then once a week at a staff meeting teach one more thing. Have the employees each take a turn explaining how to do new things on the software. In a staff meeting have the employees brainstorm specific functions that they would like the software to do and assign them to the employees and set up a timetable. Most employees take pride in becoming the expert in a particular area and explaining it to other people in the firm.

Replace hardware every two to three years. Technology is progressing at lightening speed and as soon as you purchase hardware it is immediately outdated. Many business owners don't replace hardware until it breaks, instead of having dollars budgeted each year to replace and upgrade hardware on an ongoing basis. In the 90's small businesses could purchase hardware and wait four or five years before replacing it. Today, with the continued advances in software and the ever increasing need for more memory and more speed, machines that are more than two to three years old will have trouble reading data from the newest programs. I recommend having a routine of replacing hardware every two to three years.

Don't purchase the cheapest computer. Don't purchase the cheapest computer that will do the job. You get what you pay for. One year, I purchased six new computers for my office that were on sale from a local computer store. They were about 50% of the price of most of the computers that had the same specifications. Within six months, all of the power supplies stopped working and had to be replaced. Fortunately, I had purchased an on-site warranty, but we were down three to five days for each breakdown. The part had to be ordered, delivered and then the technician had to be called and the job worked into his schedule. I learned my lesson. It is important to purchase name brand equipment with warranties and next day on-site service agreements.

Your ITC should perform regular maintenance. Once the hardware is installed and is up and running, don't stop there. It is important to have your ITC perform monthly maintenance, download updates on programs, and do performance tuning on a regular basis. Don't wait until something breaks to call him or her. Not only is it more expensive to repair when it is broken data may be lost which increases down time and profit loss.

Store all data on the server, not on workstations. When you have more than one computer workstation, a server is necessary to share data. I recommend that all data be stored on the server. Don't let employees store data on their workstations. If they get in the habit of storing "copies" on their workstation, they may accidentally update the one on their machine and not the server and then you have different versions being used within the firm. Then you have to explain to a client what happened.

Establish procedures for storing data on server. There needs to be procedures for storing data on the server, so that all employees not only follow it, but everyone can retrieve information without wasting time trying to find documents or files. When someone saves a document or file the name that they give it may make sense at the time, but later they may not remember the clever name that they gave it. Determine the drive for all data to be stored. Then determine the major categories for the main folders or areas of the firm. For example, main folders might include: Marketing, Clients, Accounting, Vendors, and Employees. Then sub-categories for folders would be generated for each category. Employees are told when documents are filed under each category and when it is appropriate to start a new folder. Someone in the firm needs to be assigned to manage these folders and approve new folders. Countless minutes and hours are spent in firms trying to find missing saved documents.

Sensitive firm data should only be accessible by management. Other folders may have specified users. All of these rights to specific folders can be set up by the ITC and explained to the network person in the office.

Set up a system for growth. It is better to setup a system that will work for 20 people than for two, so that as you grow, the systems don't have to be constantly upgraded as well. In these cases growth can be slowed and squashed. Growth can be fueled with efficient and quick response times to the marketplace.

Schedule backups of data. Since hardware and software are not 100% reliable, backups must be scheduled. At a minimum the following backups should be scheduled, an intermittent backup during the day, a differential daily backup at night, and a complete backup at least once a week. Don't overwrite the backup that was used yesterday. There needs to be at least five sets of backups, (one for each business day of the week) so that if the last backup doesn't work, then there are others available to restore. Some lost data is better than all data being lost. It is also important that backups are taken offsite each night. Some companies use an online backup system to keep data offsite. Therefore, if there is a theft or catastrophe, such as fire or storm, the data is separated from the hardware. Most contemporary backup software offers the ability to alert via e-mail (or some other means) an end-user, owner, or ITC of backup problems or failures. I strongly encourage you to purchase software with these abilities. My ITC recommends disk-image-based backup technologies rather than tape as it is really obsolete.

Test the backup. Please test the backup occasionally. Don't assume that it is doing what it is scheduled to do. One year on April 20th my hard drive crashed and nothing the ITC did would bring up the hard drive. When we inspected the backup we realized that we were missing some data. All data was supposed to be stored on my "G" drive and the program files were to be stored on my "F" drive. So the backup was scheduled to backup the "G" drive during the day and at night. Unfortunately, I found out that several programs that we installed after the backup was set up on the server, would only store data on a root directory such as "F" and not "G". The employee who installed them didn't think anything about backup and installed the programs and didn't know that the backup needed to be changed. I had to send the hard drive to a company that specialized in data recovery and spent over $3,000 to recover data that should have been at our fingertips. I also learned that only one person should install software on the computer server and workstations and that this person should also be responsible for the backups and updating computer procedures as well.

Need a log for software installation. I also learned that it was important to have a log for software installation. The log should not only indicate the drive that the program was installed on and the drive that the data was to be stored on, but also the version of the software currently installed. The name of the software company and their contact information are also important to include on the log. If you have not kept a log and want to start on there is a handy little tool called BelArc (www.belarc.com) will do a very thorough hardware and software inventory of your PCs and servers. If you're going to keep a log do so for each application and log all support calls. Indicate that the backup software is backing up this data as well. The master copy for all of the firm's software needs to be cataloged and kept under lock and key. Don't let employees borrow software to take home and try out. Not only does it violate software license rules but you may loose your master and have to repurchase the software when you need it again. Protect the firm first. There are exceptions to this rule and you should check with your ITC regarding the rules that apply to the software that you currently are using.

Request all login scripts and passwords to all programs. Another way to protect the firm is to request from the ITC person all your login scripts and passwords for all network programs. Put these in a safe place. These are owned by the firm and should be protected by the firm. ITC people come and go and the firm needs to have ready access to this information.

Select an ITC that is in the business full time. Good ITC people are hard to find. Don't take shortcuts and hire the friend of a friend who works in a large company IT department. If this person doesn't breathe and eat your type of business and then he or she probably can't anticipate your needs. I you are not a primary client then you will have to wait until they have time to address your needs. Again, your company needs to be as efficient as possible and in order to compete in today's marketplace you need an ITC who is in the business fulltime and considers you a desirable client who needs to be serviced on a timely basis. Uptime is everything and is what will give you the advantage when your competitor's systems are down. The reverse is also true.

Install anti-virus programs. Another challenge that small business owners face, is the invasion of viruses into their computer systems. How do you prevent them? There are ways to minimize the danger of viruses infiltrating your computer system. Install an anti-virus software program on all workstations and servers. A centrally managed solution works best. The virus software should be set to automatically update. Employees should be instructed to test every disk for viruses before copying them to their machine or the server. There should be a procedure for saving files from the Internet and testing before opening them at the workstation. Procedures aren't effective unless communicated to employees and then they should be reinforced on a regular basis.

Install programs to prevent spyware and pop-ups. Computers can be slowed down when spyware (also called adware or malware) attaches itself to your computer. This happens when you go to websites on the Internet and the website is set up to try to farm your data and install popup windows on your computer which uses up memory. To eliminate this spyware, you need to have software that either keeps them from having access and/or cleans up your memory and removes the popup windows. Some versions of spyware elimination software are free and have to be run manually. There are versions that can be purchased and will run continuously. Again you pay for what you get, and I recommend that you purchase the software that runs continuously and allows you to concentrate on what you do best. Many of the newer anti-virus software solutions come bundled with anti-spyware software.

Restrict instant messaging with someone outside the firm. Employers seeking to improve employee efficiency should implement policies restricting the use of instant messaging within the firm. When employees have an instant messaging software installed on their computer, it is running all of the time and utilizing memory that could be used for other programs. Also employees are distracted as they are interrupted with someone sending an instant message to them for immediate response. It is bad enough to have emails coming into the computer continuously offering distractions, but instant messages expect to be addressed immediately. When the employee stops and responds to the instant messages received from non-business sources and then returns to the task at hand, time and efficiency is lost.

Intra-company instant messaging may be ok. However, some companies utilize instant messaging within the company to communicate when employees are on the phone with clients. Some examples that may be appropriate: 1) reminder of staff meetings, 2) questions regarding other clients that can be answered with a yes or no, 3) phone calls waiting. This use of instant messaging does save the company time. It is therefore important to establish the appropriate and approved company guidelines for the use of instant messaging within the firm.

Establish procedures for email. It is also important to establish procedures for sending, receiving, saving, and storing emails. Employees need to have time limits for responding to incoming emails. Training on *Outlook* should be a priority for new employees to maximize their efficiency and time management with administrative functions. I recommend that employees have remote access to their email and to their computer whenever possible.

Set up remote access for employees. Anytime someone from the outside has remote access it is important to have security measures built into the system. Protocols and firewalls need to be established. Access to the firm's data and the ability to copy data need to be restricted. Employees should only have access to files with which they are allowed to interact. They should not be able to delete any files. An audit trail should be instigated to track any changes made and to distinguish who had made the changes. The firm should always be able to determine which employee altered files. Employees need to know this feature exists in order to deter unauthorized changes to client files.

Adopt End-User Technology Agreement. As a matter of course the company should also adopt an End-User Technology Agreement for all users/employees to read and sign which governs acceptable e-mail and Internet use, expectations of privacy, IT resource allocation, etc.

Assign someone to be the network administrator. Throughout this Chapter I have introduced the concept of having one person be assigned a number of computer hardware and software oversight functions. This person might function as your part-time network administrator. All communication with ITC should be coordinated through this person to prevent extra fees from the ITC. This network administrator will save time as all "fixes" or "how to do's" will be vetted through this person and minimize the need to contact the ITC.

The firm's computer system is the brain of the operation. The firm's computer system is the brain of the operation and without it the work of the firm will come to a screeching halt. It deserves the time and attention to set it up properly. If Marie had taken the time to set things up correctly, she would have had a more efficient firm from the beginning, and she probably would have made more money along the way.

TECHNOLOGY CHECKLIST

	Strategy	Page Ref #	Application To Your Business
1.	Time is money	91	
2.	Focus on the benefit to the firm	91	
3.	Use integrated programs	92	
4.	Make a list of what you want the programs to do	92	
5.	Consult with your ITC	92	
6.	Budget for training	92	
7.	Involve the employees in the training	93	
8.	Replace hardware every two to three years	93	
9.	Don't purchase the cheapest computer	93	
10.	Your ITC should perform regular maintenance	93	
11.	Store all data on the server, not on workstations	94	
12.	Establish procedures for storing data on server	94	
13.	Set up a system for growth	94	

	Strategy	Page Ref #	Application To Your Business
14.	Schedule backups of data	94	
15.	Test the backup	95	
16.	Need a log for software installation	95	
17.	Request all login scripts and passwords to all programs	96	
18.	Select an ITC that is in the business full time	96	
19.	Install anti-virus programs	96	
20.	Install programs to prevent spyware and pop-ups	97	
21.	Restrict instant messaging with someone outside the firm	97	
22.	Intra-company instant messaging may be ok	97	
23.	Establish procedures for email	97	
24.	Set up remote access for employees	98	
25.	Adopt End-User Technology Agreement	98	
26.	Assign someone to be the network administrator	98	
27.	The firm's computer system is the brain of the operation	98	

CHAPTER 10
Developing & Maintaining Your Most Valuable Asset: Your Business' Database

Sally has a growing business with five salespeople who each one use Microsoft Outlook as their database. Each salesperson is responsible for entering their new customers and new prospects into their database using Outlook on their computer. In addition, they must be in regular communication with the customers.

Several events have caused important company issues to service. Sally's best salesperson left the company recently and took with him the customer database, the list of prospects, and the respective status reports. She didn't have the necessary information to continue to service those customers and it took hours to rebuild the database and the prospects were lost completely. What could Sally have done differently to keep this from happening?

Your company's database is the most important asset of the company! It takes time and money to build a database and it should be valued and protected. You, the owner, are only one person, and you can come in contact with only so many people. In order for a business to grow you must duplicate yourself with employees. These employees should meet and network your business to others and gather information for the business database as well.

I know that it is scary to allow employees access to the company data but safeguards can be put in place to protect it.

Put the database on the server and restrict rights. The first thing that a company should do is locate the database on its company server and set up rights and restrictions for the employees/users. Employees should be able to add names to the database, change addresses and phone numbers, but not be able to delete or copy the database. I recommend the restriction of usage and that the database should be updated by the employees who are using it. This is efficient as they can make changes at the same time that they are talking to customers. Some companies have one person make all of the changes but this requires a system for everyone to forward the information to this one person. Although, this is one way to protect the database, it is not real time and errors can occur in between the time that the request for change is placed and when the change is actually made. I recommend that you protect the database by restricting usage rights. Allow the employees to make address changes but prevent them from making record deletions and from copying the database. Always have a journal or audit function turned on to track any changes in case you have to rebuild it.

Include everyone that you meet in the database. The database should include everyone that you meet or with whom you have with in business contact, including vendors and competitors. I once had someone ask, "why would I want to keep track of my competitors". You may need to contact them professionally about a new customer who was once theirs or regarding a non-profit board that you both serve as members. Anytime you can save time by looking up a number through the database you have made money.

Record as much information as possible to recall later. Names, phone numbers, and addresses are important, but what other information should you record? Record where you met them and something about them, the name of their spouses, their children's names and ages, their age, any likes and dislikes, and birthdays. You can't have too much information on any one contact. This information should not be in the notes, but in separate data fields that can be sorted and tracked. Therefore, you could sort for all of the customers and prospects that are interested in baseball because a news item came out that may be of interest to that population of customers.

Keep the database up to date. A database must be kept up-to-date, it is of no use, if the addresses and contact information are not correct. It won't benefit you to send something to the wrong address or to have to wait while the information is being forwarded. This lack of correct information sends the message to the customer that they are not important enough to keep track of their information.

Checklist to update all programs. Companies with more than one software program containing customer information must establish a procedure to change the address in all of them. Customers become very frustrated when their address is changed in one program and not in another program and they have to keep calling and asking you to change their address in the other programs. Employees don't want it to be their fault so they scapegoat the system or other people. This is not the message that you want communicated to your customer either. I recommend a pre-printed checklist to be completed by the person initiating the change in one program and indicate which programs have been changed and then pass along to an administrative person to change in the other programs. Since many software programs are independently developed for various industries, they may not have the ability to communicate and share data and this is required to update all of the programs at one time.

One master database that "talks to" the rest of the programs. The ideal situation is to have one master database that all of the programs "talk to" to obtain the client's information. This eliminates the need for making changes in each of the multiple programs. This may require that new software programs that are compatible be obtained and replace existing programs. It is time consuming to learn new programs but if the end result is that the company is more efficient it is worth exploring.

Use a card reader. If you have multiple people obtaining business cards at networking events, it is labor intensive to input into the database. A card reader is a wonderful piece of technology it saves key strokes and will allow you to manage your data faster. A business card is scanned by the card reader and you verify the information and make any changes and import individually or as a daily batch into your database program. An employee can be trained to add information that is written on the back of the card, to send more information on a particular product or to schedule appointments or follow-ups at particular times.

Stay in contact with newsletters. Once you have the information captured in the database, you have the ability to contact anyone on a regular basis. You can send newsletters to keep your company and your name in front of the customers and prospects. These can be e-newsletters if you have captured the email addresses. You can send newsletter by US Mail. You can send blast faxes, etc. There are many ways to stay in contact with this person and their company.

Use contact management software. I prefer database programs that are contact managers. These programs allow you to set up follow-up tickler notes for "to do's", calls, and meetings for a particular contact. The program that I have used since 2000, is ACT!(r) Contact and Customer Manager Program, currently owned by Sage Software. This program integrates with Microsoft Office for Word for letters and fax covers, Outlook for emails and WinFax for faxing through the computer. Letters, faxes, and emails are noted on the note pad for future reference. This is really important as you have other employees servicing the customers, they can review the notes and stay up to date in servicing that customer. Documents are also saved to the customer contact to be pulled up at a moment's notice. Future activities are on another screen which allows you to see anything scheduled for the future for this customer.

All of this information is at your finger tips and readily accessible by your employees for efficiency in servicing that customer. Another benefit of keeping notes when interacting with customers is that you can look up customers and see the status on projects and contacts with the customer by the employees.

Communication with your employees is improved. I frequently wonder after hours where the employees stand on projects with certain customers. I can look up the customers in the database and their recorded notes on the customer contact update me and I don't have to wait until the next business day. You are not constantly hunting them down to find out what is going on with a particular customer.

Sort by one field or multiple fields. Any field that contains data needs to be able to be sorted or recalled by that field through the database. The ability to sort by a number of fields is also important. Therefore, all individuals who live within a certain geographical location, who are interested in a particular product line and who are serviced by the same salesperson can be selected for a letter or email.

Set up groups or categories. Another way of earmarking database records is by groups or categories. I have groups for each of the non-profit boards and organizations of which I am a participant or member. I also have sub-sets for the other board members or sub-committees of which I am a member of as well. I can then send separate emails to these groups or individually addressed emails through ACT(r), which again saves time. By saving the document to the database record I can recall it without having to find a paper copy and pull a file. Anything that I can do to save current and future time is profitable.

Set up "to-do's." Setting up reminders or "to do's" is important. You can break down a project for a customer and schedule specific dates to complete these tasks in the database. Follow up "to do's" can also be scheduled, if they want you get back to them after a certain period or in a particular month this can be scheduled. These "to-do's" can be listed on the day that you need to call the customer.

Maintain the office calendar on the database. The entire office calendar can be maintained in a contact manager program or in Microsoft Outlook as well. You want the employees to have access to the entire office schedule so they can coordinate appointments for each other. This allows the facilitation of setting appointments with fellow employees without having to have numerous conversations or to track each other down. Most programs with calendar features allow you to mark certain appointments as personal and not share all of the information. Again, improving communication within the office among yourself and your employees is very important as it reduces the frustration levels for everyone.

Synchronize your database with your PDA. I am not always at my computer. I am frequently out in the field at client offices or in my car and I need my calendar and my contact phone numbers when I am out of the office. Before Personal Desk Assistants, or PDA's, I would call my assistant and ask for my calendar on a particular day, talk with my customer, and then call my assistant back to schedule it in the calendar. It took both of us to make an appointment with me. I now can synchronize my contacts and calendar with my PDA and carry it around with me. I then can schedule appointments when I am out of the office and upon returning, put the PDA in the computer cradle to synchronize with my desktop, so that appointments that I made are transferred and appointments that my office have scheduled are transferred. Occasionally there are conflicts, but very rarely and I have used less staff time and more technology instead. Some PDA's can synchronize through cellular connections and send emails and alarms from the database to you when you are away from the computer.

Backup up your database separately. Many companies have overall procedures for backing up their computer data for the whole company. I recommend that you have a backup procedure just for the database. Back up at least once a week, just the database and have someone assigned to do and verify that it is done. The owner should take home a copy of the database at least once a week, to get it off campus, in case something happens to the office or the computers. It is easier to restore your data for one program from a separate backup than to have to sift through the entire company's data to restore just one program.

Fast access to information in the database. In this fast paced world we live in the company that has the quickest access to information will have the competitive edge. With accurate, instantaneous (or close to it) information, companies can respond to the market place faster. They can contact their customers with new product lines, address industry issues, and can protect their market share by staying in front of their customer. Technology has advanced to the point that even the smallest of companies can afford database and customer management software on their desktop and laptop computers.

Well-maintained databases, keep employees productive. Keeping employees productive is a challenge for many small business owners. When the employees have to spend hours every day trying to find phone numbers and addresses of customers, prospects and vendors, the company looses money. You want to have your employees as self-sufficient as possible, but you also want to establish guidelines for company data. The database belongs to the company and the employees are just maintaining the data for the company, not the other way around.

Protected and valued asset. Now when Sally has a salesperson leave her company, she still has the customer information, the status, and the follow-up information to transition to the next sales person. By centralizing the database location and setting up procedures for all of the employees to use, the company has improved efficiency and communication in the office and the employees are less frustrated in servicing the customers. The company owns the database and it is now a valued and protected asset of the company.

YOUR BUSINESS' DATABASE CHECKLIST

	Strategy	Page Ref #	Application To Your Business
1.	Put the database on the server and restrict rights	102	
2.	Include everyone that you meet in the database	102	
3.	Record as much information as possible to recall later	102	
4.	Keep the database up to date	103	
5.	Checklist to update all programs	103	
6.	One master database that "talks to" the rest of the programs	103	
7.	Use a card reader	103	
8.	Stay in contact with newsletters	104	
9.	Use contact management software	104	
10.	Communication with your employees is improved	104	
11.	Sort by one field or multiple fields	104	
12.	Set up groups or categories	105	
13.	Set up "to-do's"	105	

	Strategy	Page Ref #	Application To Your Business
14.	Maintain the office calendar on the database	105	
15.	Synchronize your database with your PDA	105	
16.	Backup up your database separately	106	
17.	Fast access to information in the database	106	
18.	Well-maintained databases, keep employees productive	106	
19.	Protected and valued asset	107	

CHAPTER 11
Marketing

Terry opened a bakery and pastry shop in a downtown shopping district. He was a very good pastry chef and believed that when customers tried his pastries and deserts they would be so pleased that they would spread the word and he would be very successful. Therefore, he did not spend money to advertise or promote his business. After six months he was struggling to pay his bills, wondering what he did wrong and what he should do going forward. Terry didn't know if he could save his business. What should Terry do?

Don't assume customers will find you. The worst thing that a business owner like Terry can do is to assume that customers will find you and that they will know what you are selling. Even if they know what you do, tell them again, because they will forget.

Research the market place and competition. Prior to the shop opening, Terry should have researched the market place and determined who his competition would be and their level of expertise. If he could figure out a niche or a way to distinguish himself from them he could rise above competition. For example, he might provide products that the competition doesn't, such as wedding cakes and fancy deserts.

Identify complimentary businesses and explore cross-marketing opportunities. He also needs to determine if there are any local businesses that his service can compliment and if they could cross-refer to each other. For example, he could team up with a popular coffee company and they could promote each other's products. Terry could sell their coffee in his shop. He might even be able to provide pastries and deserts to other stores in the area.

Market to wholesale business to market your services or products. Prior to opening the store he should have made a list of the local restaurants and visited the owners of each one to determine their pastry and desert needs. He could have presented each of them a proposal to supply them with pastries and deserts on a daily basis for their customers. This may generate a repeating core business on a monthly basis. If this business could be developed to cover his basic overhead, then the shop business and weddings etc could provide his profit. You don't have to sell to the end consumer 100% of the time to be successful in business.

Terry could also confer with the catering businesses which are not associated with a particular restaurant. Caterers need pastries and/or deserts in almost all of their jobs.

It doesn't matter what industry you are in, it is important to identify other businesses that could use your goods and services or businesses with which you could cross-refer business.

Join merchant and business associations. Terry's shop is in a downtown shopping district that probably has a downtown merchant's association. Now he should visit and join the association. He should meet the leaders and obtain a list of their activities. There may be events that the downtown merchants association sponsors as a group with group marketing, instead of each business promoting itself individually. This should be more effective and he could plan his promotions for each of these events. He could plan a grand opening around one of these events, when more people would already be visiting the downtown area.

Join the Chamber of Commerce. Terry should contact the local Chamber of Commerce and learn about their activities and consider joining. By participating in committees and networking activities he could get to know the members, pass out flyers and make announcements about his business grand opening and daily, weekly and monthly specials that he might have.

Capture contacts and enter into database. Every business card that Terry collects should be entered into a database. He needs to record how they met and something about them, for example their birthday and favorite desert. He could email each person in the database announcements about the weekly specials or new items as they are introduced at the shop. He could send each person a birthday card with a gift certificate for a desert. This would get the person to come into the shop and hopefully buy something else besides picking out their complimentary desert. Hopefully, after they see the shop and all of the items that Terry offers, they will be back to buy pastries and deserts in the future. I have an entire chapter devoted to using databases. See Chapter 10, *Databases*.

Establish a membership program. Terry could start a Desert Club with membership cards that provide benefits. For example, with each desert purchase of $10 or more, the card is punched. After 10 punches, then the member receives a free desert. This promotes return visits and helps develop a loyal customer base.

Send out press releases for grand opening, new product lines, etc. Before Terry's grand opening, he should distribute press releases to the local newspapers, magazines, radio and TV stations. He should contact the local newspaper food editor and talk with them about the grand opening, invite them to a pre-opening sampling of special pastries and deserts. If they are impressed, they might write a story right before the grand opening or the day of the grand opening and give Terry free publicity. Every time a new product line or special desert is offered at the shop a press release should be done. Terry should invite this food editor on a regular basis to his shop.

Ask for Testimonials. As customers visit the shop and come back to buy more goods, Terry should ask them for testimonials. He could take their picture with a digital camera and have them write out their testimonial. If Terry had a digital video camera that could be brought out very quickly to video the testimonial that would be ideal.

Establish website. Terry needs to have a website to promote his business, provide directions to the shop, offer email subscriptions to a newsletter and a calendar of events. A monthly newsletter with simple recipes for quick deserts for busy Moms would be a way to attract new customers and compile a customer list to continue to market other goods and services. Terry could offer sponsored links on the website to other complimentary businesses. He could also have pictures of specific deserts and pastries for customers to see. He could have an order form on the website for pastry and desert orders and the date to pick up from the shop. Other items to include in the website would be daily, weekly, and monthly specials, as well as bios on key personnel in the business and press releases or articles that have been published about the business.

Publish articles in magazines. Terry could offer to write weekly or monthly articles for a food magazine. He should frame any of these published articles and write-ups from the food editors that promote his business. These should be proudly displayed for customers to see.

Be active in community. Terry should be active in community and government issues and activities. Not only is it important to give back to the community, it is an excellent way to meet community leaders and work side by side on issues or events. This facilitates important friendships and business references.

Nominate business for awards. After a few years he could either apply or have other community members nominate his business for chamber of commerce and community awards. It is important for the business to not only be active in the community but receive the recognition that it deserves. Many times the selection committees do not have many applicants for these awards. People are busy and forget to take time nominate deserving businesses. These awards are usually presented at large meetings and receive publicity in the local papers. The awards should not be the goal of the community service but are an added benefit if Terry has a passion and is committed to being active in the community.

Deliver speeches. Many local civic clubs meet weekly and are looking for community leaders to provide short speeches each week. If Terry can deliver speeches about his profession to these groups it would be an excellent way of becoming known as an expert in his field. Members of his organization may be more inclined to shop at his store.

Offer classes to customers. If the shop is large enough and he planned ahead in the design of the shop, he could offer cooking classes. This is an excellent way of bringing potential customers into the shop to learn from him and discover his expertise and have fun as well. They may try the items at home and have some success. Many customers will purchase items from him in the future and will tell others about the fun experience that they had with his store.

Direct mail. Another way that Terry could promote his business would be to send out oversized postcards or flyers advertising events such as open houses, holiday goods, etc. to his target market. His target market may be surrounding neighborhoods and businesses. There are a number of companies that provide mailing lists with various criteria: income, zip codes, price of house etc.

Survey customers as you meet them. Everyone who comes into the shop should be asked how they heard about the shop. Notes should be taken to track the advertising and marketing methods which are working for Terry. Then the various programs can be refined, enhanced, or deleted so that resources are allocated to the things that work.

Develop a marketing budget. Terry should develop a marketing budget and a specific plan for pre-opening and on-going marketing with associated dollar amounts. Someone in the business, if not Terry, should be assigned to make sure that the marketing plan is implemented.

Consider hiring a public relations firm. Terry may not feel comfortable doing all of the items that I've discussed, however he needs to do something. If he doesn't know how or want to market his business or if he wants advise on the best ways to market his business, he should consider hiring a public relations firm. These firms can help him get his articles published, issue press releases, obtain speaking engagements, and offer other marketing strategies.

Implement a targeted marketing plan. Most of these marketing strategies can be applied to other industries as well. The most important thing for any business besides providing the best quality product or service for a reasonable price is to implement a targeted marketing plan. Terry will find that a well prepared plan produces sweet rewards.

MARKETING CHECKLIST

	Strategy	Page Ref #	Application To Your Business
1.	Don't assume customers will find you	111	
2.	Research the market place and competition	111	
3.	Identify complimentary businesses and explore cross-marketing opportunities	111	
4.	Market to wholesale business to market your services or products	112	
5.	Join merchant and business associations	112	
6.	Join the Chamber of Commerce	112	
7.	Capture contacts and enter into database	112	
8.	Establish a membership program	113	
9.	Send out press releases for grand opening, new product lines, etc.	113	
10.	Ask for Testimonials	113	
11.	Establish website	113	
12.	Publish articles in magazines	114	

	Strategy	Page Ref #	Application To Your Business
13.	Be active in community	114	
14.	Nominate business for awards	114	
15.	Deliver speeches	114	
16.	Offer classes to customers	114	
17.	Direct mail	115	
18.	Survey customers as you meet them	115	
19.	Develop a marketing budget	115	
20.	Consider hiring a public relations firm	115	
21.	Implement a targeted marketing plan	115	

CHAPTER 12
Internet Marketing & Websites

Dan has a small novelty gift company and wants to explore expanding his company. He has heard about the Internet and he wants to set up a website and have customers order merchandise on line. He needs to know his options and the things to consider so that he can be as successful as possible in a short period of time.

Advantages of using the Internet. The advantages of using the Internet include:

1) Minimal marketing costs. You may have to purchase someone's time to design your website, set up your website and perform periodic maintenance and updates to the website. However, this is still significantly cheaper than the historic ways of marketing by using direct mail, radio and TV, and print ads.

2) You don't have to purchase the product or display the product until it is listed and sold online.

3) Sending emails and having a high ranking on the search engines is also a small cost to advertise your website and products.

4) The communication by email or a search on the web that produces your website provides for instant delivery. The postal service takes several days and there are paper and printing costs as well.

5) Your website can be updated instantly when there are changes in laws or changes in procedures that affect your customers.

6) You can try new ideas on the Internet and find out if they are marketable without spending a lot of money.

Select your domain name. The first step in setting up your website is selecting your domain name. Before you choose your entity's name, search to determine that it is also available as a domain name or something close to it. You should consider the following ideas in selecting your domain name:

1) Simple is best. Hard to spell names should be avoided. Customers will misspell the name and they will never get to your website. To avoid this, you will have to purchase every variation of the name and have them forwarded to your website.

2) Make it catchy or easy for the customer to remember and they will be more likely to visit the site and do business with you.

Select a company to host your website. The company needs to be reliable, so ask for references and services offered. They need to have limited network down time and maintenance issues and be reasonably priced. The cheapest isn't always the best in business. Once your business depends on your website, if the website goes down, your business goes down. Some industries have companies that will offer reduced monthly hosting costs and provide industry specific services if you are a member of a particular industry. Review industry trade magazines and trade organization websites to find this type of company.

Website templates. You don't have to have someone design your website from scratch. There are companies that sell templates that already have graphics and page formats pre-set. You can modify the template to show your company information and tailor it to suit your company's needs and products. You can upload documents, pictures, and text as needed. Some templates are so easy to use that you can literally buy the template in the morning, have it modified, and your website can be up and live in the afternoon.

Software programs can modify and design websites. You don't have to learn computer languages to modify your website anymore. There are software programs that ask you questions and offer menu selections, similar to word processing, which walk you through creating and modifying your website.

Upload pictures and graphics. Make your website colorful and interesting with pictures and graphics. Put pictures of your company staff on the website and allow them to come alive for the customer, which will make working with your company a little more personal. You want to connect with a customer who you have never met and this is one way of accomplishing just that.

Calculators or worksheets. Consider putting calculators or worksheets on your website for customers to use. On my website, I have financial calculators, so that clients and potential clients can estimate their retirement income and then determine if they are saving enough to accumulate the required assets to generate their desired retirement income.

Easy to navigate website. It is so frustrating to be told that the information that you need right now is somewhere on this website and you can't find it. The navigation tabs on the website need to be terms which make sense to the end user and not just the web designer. Have a customer or two review your website before it goes live to give you feedback from an end user prospective. When I was growing up, my Mother would tell me to look up words I didn't know how to spell in the dictionary, but I had to know how to pronounce them and spell them to look them up. Don't make me, as your customer; have to know something that I don't know in order to use your website. The most user-friendly sites are ones that have several ways to navigate them, with tabs across the top and along the side of each page, besides having a site map available, and a key word search of the website that can be used in the event that a user still can't find what they need.

Testimonials. Since companies aren't having personal contact with the customer through the website, many companies request testimonials from satisfied customers and they receive permission to post them on the website. This gives the potential new customer comments from satisfied customers to consider in their decision to purchase goods and services from the particular company's website.

Audio and video instructions, introductions and testimonials. Websites traditionally use only a visual mode of communication with pictures that must be seen and words that must be read. Adding audio or video combines the visual and the verbal and interests the customer more than other visual websites. The customers tend to stay on your website longer and the longer they stay on your website, the more likely they will be to make purchases from your company. Ways to use the audio and video include:

1) Providing ordering instructions,
2) Educating the customer about a particular product,
3) Introducing the owners or staff and explaining their qualifications in a personable way,
4) Videoing testimonials. This is more interesting than just reading a testimonial, and will likely have more of an impact.

Audio and video are more expensive than traditional websites but the benefits of customer utilization and purchases may far outweigh the costs and should be considered.

Meta tags are important. When your website is designed, you need to include in the Meta tag as many key words as possible for the search engines to recognize and use when customers search for these key words. Doing this will make the link to your website appear higher up on the list that is returned in response to a keyword search on the major search engines, which will increase your website's traffic.

Register with search engines. Register initially with the search engines after you have the website completed. You must continue to monitor your location on the search results and tweak your website by adding more content and information in order to raise your level on the search results.

Purchase ad words and advertised spots on search result pages. You can bid for the cost per click for certain words in online ad space. The more commonly the word is used by Internet searches, the more expensive it can be per click. In theory, the more 'hits' that your website receives, the greater the chance that customers will purchase your goods and services. If they don't visit your website, it is impossible to sell them anything. The cost vs. benefit of this advertising must be evaluated for expensive words, but depending on the sales prices of your goods and services, it may be worth it. On the right side of and at the top of the Internet search pages sometimes highlighted in blue or yellow, are purchased ads for key words. These may charge a base rate and a charge per click or just a charge per click. Again, the key is to generate traffic to your website.

Website statistics. There are also companies that sell access to software which monitors your website and tracks the number of clicks, from where the visitor originated, and where the visitor traveled on your website. Through a tool like this, you can discover what marketing is working and where to modify it. Many hosting companies offer this through their services.

Articles and industry updates added to your website weekly and monthly. Continue to update your website by adding articles and industry updates. These articles may be created by you or purchased through industry ghost writers with permission. Don't post anything that has copyright protection without giving the author full credit and obtaining their permission. If there are any questions about author permission or copyright licensing, you can put a link on your website to the location of the article on the other author's website, instead of posting the text itself.

Don't let the website look stale. Don't let the information on your website look stale, or as if it never changes. Create reasons for your customers to come to your website. Customers like to be educated — not sold. By learning from the articles and other educational material on your website, customers will be more likely to trust your company and make their next purchase from you.

Post popular links that your customers may request. Again, you want your customer to look to your company as the expert in your industry, and to feel that they should visit your website first for any information they need. Provide Internet links for their convenience to the most popular industry sites that may come in handy. For example, as a CPA, my website has links to the IRS and the State of Georgia, as well as the SBA and local vendors for various services that my clients may need.

Vendor links. Negotiate with vendors to have their link on your website and your link on their website. Negotiate referral fees when appropriate. If you are happy with the vendor and your customers like you, they will probably like the vendor as well. Selecting vendors is time consuming and customers appreciate referrals. Make sure that your vendors understand the responsibility that they take on in receiving a referral. If they do not do a good job it could be a reflection on you and you could lose the customer, or vice versa. Offering links on your website for other companies can elevate your listing by the search engines to a higher listing when potential customers do searches. Clicks on this link can be tracked, so that if the customer buys something on the other company's website, there is a record of the link or site referral. This way, if you are to be paid a referral fee you will have the information to get paid.

Easier to sell additional products to existing customers than to develop and sell to new potential customers. Once you have obtained a customer that has purchased goods or services from your website, stay connected to them through auto responders and emails of new or featured products. It is easier to sell additional products and services to existing customers than to develop and sell products to new potential customers.

Offer information to visitors of your website and capture their email addresses. Build your email list, it is very valuable. Be careful to obtain and use email addresses in a manner that does not violate anti-spam laws. Once someone has become connected with your website, they are interested in your products and services. Stay in contact with them through regular emails. Give them value in your emails; do not just send emails to send emails. If there is no value in your emails, they will be deleted before they are even read and the customer may even be deterred by what they perceive as 'spamming'.

Establish alliance partners. Negotiate with other companies to become alliance partners, and have them promote your product through their email list for a referral fee. You may do the same for their products and receive a referral fee as well.

Entire catalogs of merchandise can be put on the web. Entire catalogs of merchandise can be put on your website and you don't even have to have a real store to display the merchandise. Pictures of each product with dimensions and features can be loaded on the website and customers can shop from the convenience of their home.

Order online and pick up in a store. Online prices tend to be cheaper, but shipping costs have to be added to the price to determine the total cost. Additionally, you have to wait until the item is delivered to your doorstep in the next week or even longer. Some stores are offering online purchasing with in store pick up. This can be profitable for both the business and the customer because the customer can get the cheaper price without having to pay for shipping or waiting to have it delivered. The store gets business from people who don't want to have to search the store for what they want.

Post products facts and frequently asked questions and answers. When your customer is evaluating your product for purchase they may have questions. Online, there isn't a clerk standing in front of them to whom they can pose their questions. A list of frequently asked questions and answers posted next to the product picture on the website would help the customer in most cases. These questions could be compiled from questions that customers have already asked or that the company can anticipate based on similar products. The customer still needs to be able to contact the company with any questions that are not addressed on the website. So make sure that the customer can email for sales support on every page.

Information about the company and staff. Although the primary reason that the customer is visiting your website is to learn about your products and services, they may want to know the qualifications and experience level of your company and staff. Post pictures and qualifications and email addresses of staff. List the company contact information including mailing address and phone and fax numbers.

Feature staff of the month. Select a staff member each month to feature or highlight and put their picture on the home page and share more of their business accomplishments and more about them personally than in their short bio. This will make them seem more real to your customers.

Post documents and information that is frequently requested by your customers. When your customers ask for specific documents and information that you have posted on your website, your staff can point them to the website for downloading and/or printing this information. This will save staff time and free them up for other duties in the office. Keep in mind, however, that it is still a good idea to have a few hard copies on hand in the store or office because some customers may not be willing to seek out the documents on their own.

Project management updates. Some companies are using their website to update their customers on projects that are in process. The customer logs into a secure part of the website and retrieves their list of projects that are in process with the company. They can check for updates and expected completion dates. Notes can be listed for the customer to provide more information in specific areas. A log is kept of all activities on the project, including who worked on the individual tasks and progress and completion dates. This method of communicating provides faster communication to the customer because they don't have to wait for a return phone call and they can check even after normal business hours.

Don't forget you are still dealing with people. Although the Internet is an efficient way of communicating, your company should not forget that you are still dealing with people and they should attempt to make personal contact on whenever possible to keep the customer connected and happy with the personal service of the company.

Event advertisement and registration. If your company produces events for customers, your website can offer information about the event and the opportunity for your customers to register online. If there is a fee for the event your website can accept payments online as well.

Shopping carts. To encourage your customers to place orders on your website accept a variety of methods of payment. These methods can include most or all major credit cards, a bank draft for the entire balance, or a set series of payments. Your web designer doesn't have to create a shopping cart from scratch, there are companies that provide the secured encryption and websites for processing these payments for a base monthly fee and a per transaction fee.

Secure member services. Many organizations have websites that offer special member services. After the member logs in to the members' only section of the website, special information and services are made available to the member. This provides more timely information than trying to contact the executive director and his or her staff to obtain most requested information. It also reduces the staff time required to service the membership and allows the staff to provide more or better services that require human input.

Create a presence on the Internet even if you don't have a customer base. By driving traffic to your website, you can create a presence on the Internet even if you don't have a customer base. Using the search engines, providing content on the website for the search engines to record key words, using the key words in the Meta Tags, buying ad words and ad space per key word and per click, as previously discussed, you can drive traffic to your website.

Offer e-newsletters. Now that you have traffic to your website, invite the visitors to subscribe to your weekly or monthly e-newsletter. Use auto responders to send an automatic message acknowledging the subscription and introducing the e-newsletter and when they can expect to receive them and what topics will be included each month or week. By having regular email contact with the visitors and the customers, it will keep them connected with your website and your company, as well as build your email client list.

Archive old newsletters by topic. Archive old newsletters by topic on your website. Your customers can retrieve them whenever they need them. You can point customers to your website to learn more about these topics at their convenience.

Let technology work for you while you sleep. Your website can attract visitors and sell your products and services without your participation. These customers can be located around the world. Use a shopping cart package to accept payments from the order and use auto responders to email the customer a receipt for their order. Capture the customer's contact information for your database for future follow up. Use a fulfillment center to fill the order and ship it to your customer. Once everything is set up and the inventory is at the fulfillment center, you can answer emails anywhere with Internet access. You can make money from the beach, in the mountains, at home, and in the office too!

INTERNET MARKETING & WEBSITES CHECKLIST

	Strategy	Page Ref #	Application To Your Business
1.	Advantages of using the Internet	119	
2.	Select your domain name	120	
3.	Select a company to host your website	120	
4.	Website templates	121	
5.	Software programs can modify and design websites	121	
6.	Upload pictures and graphics	121	
7.	Calculators or worksheets	121	
8.	Easy to navigate website	121	
9.	Testimonials	122	
10.	Audio and video instructions, introductions and testimonials	122	
11.	Meta tags are important	122	
12.	Register with search engines	122	
13.	Purchase ad words and advertising spots on search result pages	123	

	Strategy	Page Ref #	Application To Your Business
14.	Website statistics	123	
15.	Articles and industry updates added to your website weekly and monthly	123	
16.	Don't let the website look stale	123	
17.	Post popular links that your customers may request	123	
18.	Vendor links	124	
19.	Easier to sell additional products to existing customers than to develop and sell to new potential customers	124	
20.	Offer information to visitors of your website and capture their email addresses	124	
21.	Establish alliance partners	125	
22.	Entire catalogs of merchandise can be put on the web	125	
23.	Order online and pick up in a store	125	
24.	Post products facts and frequently asked questions and answers	125	

	Strategy	Page Ref #	Application To Your Business
25.	Information about the company and staff	125	
26.	Feature staff of the month	126	
27.	Post documents and information that is frequently requested by your customers	126	
28.	Project management updates	126	
29.	Don't forget you are still dealing with people	126	
30.	Event advertisement and registration	126	
31.	Shopping carts	126	
32.	Member services	127	
33.	Create a presence on the Internet even if you don't have a customer base	127	
34.	Offer e-newsletters	127	
35.	Archive old newsletters by topic	127	
36.	Let technology work for you while you sleep	127	

CHAPTER 13
Accounting System

Jim started a restaurant business and decided he didn't have time to learn an accounting software program. He did have a cash register with food, beverage and alcohol sales keys. He used hand spreadsheets for checking out each day. Each column had to be totaled on the adding machine. The credit card sales were difficult to track as the credit card companies deducted their fee from each deposit. He paid for some deliveries out of the cash drawer and sometimes the receipts were put into the drawer.

Jim has found that running a restaurant takes a lot of time and energy and there is little time for record keeping. He has also found that he needs more information to help him manage his business profitably. He knows that food costs vary daily and without good information he will not know how to price his menu. Jim is loosing money. What should he to do?

Need accounting software from the beginning. Jim needs help. He needs to use technology as much as possible General ledger accounting programs such as Intuit's QuickBooks or Microsoft's Small Business Accounting are easy to use and would help Jim simplify his record keeping and retain key information about his business. Jim has learned that it is important to have a good accounting system. If set up properly from the beginning, these programs are a good investment and indispensable management tools.

Implement daily procedures. By implementing a few simple daily cash handling and accounting procedures Jim can have the information he needs to manage his business.

Download cash register into accounting software. The ideal situation for Jim would be if his cash register information were able to be downloaded directly into the accounting software program daily. If this is not possible, a printout from the cash register or the totals by category should be recorded at the end of each day. These totals should be input into the accounting software program on a daily basis.

Don't pay for deliveries out of cash drawer. Jim needs to exercise more control over the cash drawer and should stop paying cash for deliveries out of the cash drawer. Accounts should be set up with each vendor and monthly statements should be submitted to Jim. Sometimes as a new business it is difficult to obtain business accounts. Jim should write a check for each delivery and leave the cash in the drawer for sales only.

Prepare daily deposits. Jim should also prepare daily deposits that tie to the daily sales less credit card sales. He may only go to the bank twice a week but daily deposits need to be prepared to tie to the daily receipts. He should make sure that all deposits are made by the end of the month. This will make it easier to balance his bank statement. The last day of the month's deposit should be made as soon after the end of the month as possible. This should be recorded in the accounting system on the day it was earned not the day it was deposited. This will enable the month's receipts to be recorded in the accounting system properly.

Establish the credit card charge procedures. The credit card machine should be batched at the end of each day. This will enable the day's credit card receipts to match the bank statement. Make sure that the credit card companies bill you at the end of the month and that they don't subtract their fee from each deposit. If they deduct their fee each time it is difficult to balance the bank with the accounting system.

Record vendor invoices as received. As vendor invoices are received they should be recorded into the accounting system and the due date recorded. This will allow the owner to plan for cash flow and know when invoices are coming due to be paid.

Determine cost of goods sold. By recording expenses and receipts daily Jim can examine his food costs with his receipts. A separate analysis for each food item on the menu should be done on a weekly basis. The cost of each dish and the labor to prepare must be reviewed. If Jim is targeting 30% for food costs, he needs to divide the food costs by .30 to determine the sales price. I would use the average food costs for the last month and add 5% to the sales price, so that he doesn't have to change the prices every month. If the food costs change significantly and it looks as though the costs are going to stay at that price, then menu prices need to change accordingly. Don't worry, your competition is having the same problem, if you don't react fast enough, you won't be in business long enough for it to matter.

Manage your business. Businesses need to be managed. In one of my graduate classes, I was told that managing is like taking a blob of play-dough and squeezing it in your hand. You have most of it inside your hand. But there are small amounts that slip out between your fingers. Then you let go and then re-squeeze and then you have about the same amount inside your hand. Some of the parts that slipped out before are now inside your hand and then other parts have slipped between your fingers this time.

The act of managing is squeezing and letting go and hoping that at some point you have had all of the parts of the business inside your hand. It has been my experience that this is true. If you realize that you can't stay on top of every aspect of your business all of the time and you have a process for touching all parts at some time during the month, then you can focus on the parts at hand at that moment.

Review financial statements monthly. You need information to manage your business. No matter how much you are involved in your business, taking time to review the actual financial statements will almost always give you an 'a-ha' moment, something that you didn't realize was happening in your business. I recommend that you review the financial statements at least monthly. Make sure that the percentage of income is listed next to each income and expense item on the income statement. I recommend running a report that compares this year's income statement with last year's income statement. Also, run a report that compares the actual income statement with your budget. Note differences between the actual income and expenses compared with the budget and explain them. After reviewing these reports, make modifications to your business so that you can be more profitable.

Establish a budget. I mentioned the word budget in the previous paragraph. This is probably the best tool of any business and is probably the hardest for a business owner to sit down and prepare. Perhaps it is because they would rather be running their business, exercising their expertise. Maybe it is because they will have to make decisions in which they will be held accountable in the future. Or maybe, they don't know what their costs will be. It is difficult to reach a goal that has not been set. It is hard to communicate to employees what they are expected to do without financial goals by which to measure them. Maybe it takes precious time and it is put off by the business owner because no one is putting pressure on him or her to complete it. See Chapter 2, *Business Plans and Budgets*.

Take time to plan for the next year. When should you as a business owner plan? October should be the time of the year that you review the previous nine months and look at the projected last 3 months of the year and then plan for the next year. In my practice I have noticed that every time a client takes time to do this they are surprised to learn that they actually attained goals that had eluded them in the past. When you take time to plan it pays you over and over. Yet it is the one thing that we know we should do and yet we don't.

Budgets are learning tools. Budgets, although they are tedious, are wonderful learning tools. By reviewing your business history, and researching other businesses in your industry on the Internet, you can determine what you should be spending on each expense item. Then you can decide how much profit you want to make and set your prices.

Review business history to determine places to cut costs. By reviewing your business history, you can determine the actual cost of each expense item. Determine if there are places that you can reduce the cost.

Re-evaluate cell phone contracts and costs and the cost for land telephone lines. For example, cell phone costs should be reviewed each quarter, the cell phone companies are constantly changing plans and with the ability to transfer your phone number between carriers, you can change carriers and keep your phone number. Land lines with telephone carriers are changing periodically and should be reviewed at least annually to determine the best plan for local and long distance calls.

Review insurance policy provisions and costs. Insurance costs should be reviewed annually to see if coverage needs to be increased and to determine if you are paying the least cost for the best coverage for your company. Replacement cost is a preferable option to make sure that your company can replace the item with the insurance money. As you add new equipment, make sure that the coverage is increased.

Review your bank relationship and bank charges. Bank service charges should be monitored. If your bank charges for little things, shop around, find a bank that is small business friendly and wants your business. When you visit with the banker, get to know him or her. This person can make a big difference in your business life. Set up a credit line, even if you don't need it right now. This will ease the pain of short term cash flow crunches.

Renew the dues and subscriptions that you receive value. Review dues and subscriptions and determine if you are receiving value for each organization and magazine. Only renew the ones that are providing either education or good business contacts and business. When you are just starting out, it is important to join a number of organizations and network as much as possible. After a year or two, pairing back is appropriate when you find out what works for you and your business.

Re-evaluate equipment leases. Review any equipment leases and decide if you still need the equipment and whether it is time to exercise the payout option or to replace it at the end of the lease with purchased equipment. I leased my postage equipment when I started one of my businesses and after a couple of years, discovered it was only a couple of hundred dollars to purchase it and yet I was paying $46 per month to rent it. I wouldn't have known it, if I had not asked.

Review repairs and determine replacement costs. Are you spending too much money on repairs? You replace items that are costing you too much in repairs and in down time. Review each year and budget in the cost to replace as needed.

Negotiate utility costs. Utilities were once an expense that you couldn't do much about. I have found that these costs are negotiable now too. Call the utility company and ask about their different plans and find the one that best suites your business and saves you the most money. This should be done at least once a year. I would check the electricity before summer and the gas before winter.

Establish travel and entertainment policies and compare to actual expenses. Travel and entertainment budgets are tricky. Employees need to be provided guidelines for dinners out of town, etc. Business owners may splurge in this department as well. As long as the company is doing well no one seems to care. However, when business is tight, this area should be tightened as well. I would budget the most reasonable amount in this department to get the job done and still enjoy your self without going overboard. Then if you exceed budget expectations in net income, then splurge.

Monitor labor costs and budget for employee benefits. Labor costs vary with the type of business. In small businesses, each employee must wear multiple hats and are critical to the success of the business. Each employee must provide a service to the business or generate sales. Review industry and local salary statistics, to make sure that you are compensating your employees properly so that you don't loose them. Turnover is expensive. Include in the budget expansion costs and the adding of new employees, including fringe benefits and payroll tax costs. It takes 60 to 90 days for an employee to start paying for themselves.

Budget for a bookkeeper. Budgeting for a bookkeeper is always hard for a business owner to do. This person is always considered a non-revenue generating employee and harder to justify. I have found that this person almost always pays for him/herself rather quickly because they free up the owner to do what they do best in the business. This person will ask questions about invoices and save money finding accounts payable billing mistakes. This person can decrease the time between the company services being rendered and being billed to improve cash flow. Not to mention a bookkeeper provides timely financial information for the business owner to review. When you have access to financial information on a timely basis you can make changes in your business strategy and direction quickly. This will allow you to stay competitive and to be more profitable.

Bill your customers as often as possible. Many companies wait until the end of the month to do billing. I recommend doing billing weekly if not daily. This decreases the time between the services or product being sold and the time the customer or client receives the invoice. It starts the pay clock running as well.

Set up accounts receivable procedures for payment terms and collection. To encourage prompt payment offer discounts for payment within 10 days and charge interest for over 30 days. You are not a bank and you should charge interest when your customer or clients treat you as one. Remember you have the ability to waive the interest if you desire. However, if you waive it you set a precedent and it will be harder to collect in the future with that client. Customers or clients are like children, they will push until you push back. They won't pay until they understand the consequences of not paying. It costs money to track receivables and to follow up and collect them so set up systems to manage them. If you have discounts due in 10 days send an email at eight days to remind them they have two days left in discount period. At 20 days, send an email to remind them they have 10 days before interest will be assessed. At 31 days send statements with interest and follow up with a phone call. At 45 notify them they will be forwarded to collection agency if you do not have payment in full within 10 days. At 60 days forward them to collection agency or file small claims action in court.

If your customers or clients have legitimate issues and are trying to pay and are staying in contact with you, then you may want to extend the timeframe before collection action is taken.

Set up customer files by customer. File a copy of the customer or client billing invoices in numerical order in a file by month. File a copy of the invoices in the customer or client billing folder. Note all conversations with the client in the billing folder or in their folder in the database. It is important to follow through with collection action if warranted.

Set up vendor files by vendor. After inputting accounts payable vendor invoices into the accounting system, file alphabetically by vendor until paid.

Then file by vendor, not by month. I find that clients who have filed invoices by month paid have had a hard time retrieving the invoice later. With vendor files, you can pull the file and have all of the invoices for that vendor to review and you can see historical charges over time. By reviewing the amount paid per vendor each year you may be able to renegotiate contracts to receive lower prices.

An accounting system allows you to manage your business more competitively and profitably. If Jim sets up an accounting system and implements the processes I have described, he will know the costs of his business are and manage his business more competitively and more profitably.

ACCOUNTING SYSTEMS CHECKLIST

	Strategy	Page Ref #	Application To Your Business
1.	Need accounting software from the beginning	133	
2.	Implement daily procedures	134	
3.	Download cash register into accounting software	134	
4.	Don't pay for deliveries out of cash drawer	134	
5.	Prepare daily deposits	134	
6.	Establish the credit card charge procedures	134	
7.	Record vendor invoices as received	134	
8.	Determine cost of goods sold	135	
9.	Manage your business	135	
10.	Review financial statements monthly	135	
11.	Establish a budget	136	
12.	Take time to plan for the next year	136	
13.	Budgets are learning tools	136	
14.	Review business history to determine places to cut costs	136	

	Strategy	Page Ref #	Application To Your Business
15.	Re-evaluate cell phone contracts and costs and the cost for land telephone lines	136	
16.	Review insurance policy provisions and costs	137	
17.	Review your bank relationship and bank charges	137	
18.	Renew the dues and subscriptions that you receive value	137	
19.	Re-evaluate equipment leases	137	
20.	Review repairs and determine replacement costs	137	
21.	Negotiate utility costs	138	
22.	Establish travel and entertainment policies and compare to actual expenses	138	
23.	Monitor labor costs and budget for employee benefits	138	
24.	Budget for a bookkeeper	138	
25.	Bill your customers as often as possible	139	

	Strategy	Page Ref #	Application To Your Business
26.	Set up accounts receivable procedures for payment terms and collection	139	
27.	Set up customer files by customer	139	
28.	Set up vendor files by vendor	139	
29.	An accounting system allows you to manage your business more competitively and profitably	140	

CHAPTER 14
Managing Cash Flow

Clara started her own consulting business and quickly found that she had a number of customers. The company grew rapidly and she hired employees and spent money freely to grow her business. She didn't always have time to keep her books up to date, so she checked her company bank balance on the Internet each day. She used credit cards to charge business and personal expenses and soon found that she could not pay them off when the bills came due. She began to find it difficult to "make payroll" or have the money in the bank to pay her employees. Vendors and creditors started calling her to ask when she could make her bills and payments. She was afraid to open her mail. She was feeling unbelievable financial pressure and didn't know what had gone wrong or what she could do to fix it.

Know where you stand at all times. It does take time to keep your books up to date on accounting software. But it takes more time to use manual systems that only attempt to know where you stand; they are hit-and-miss at best. With a manual system, if you find that you missed something, it has already become a crisis situation that you have to scramble to fix. Other opportunities to make money may be lost as the crisis usually comes when other deadlines are upon you. Time itself can't be managed but how you spend your time can be managed and prioritized with careful planning. Make your bookkeeping a priority by keeping current.

Bank balance is not your book cash balance. Even though Clara checked her bank balance at the bank each day, it doesn't give her the available balance per her books. It doesn't account for checks and deposits outstanding. For her to use that bank balance she would need to subtract her outstanding checks and debits and add her outstanding deposits and credits. To do this on a daily basis is very time consuming. If her books are up to date she can use this correct balance instead.

Anticipate cash flow problems. You need to anticipate cash flow problems and have time to work out solutions. By monitoring your books and cash flow reports, you can anticipate cash flow problems. When you see billings increase and staff overtime increase you know that you may be short on payroll the next payroll payday. If you notice a loss on the books for a month using the accrual method, this will probably cause cash flow problems the next month. Monitor sales and know the minimum sales required to reach your break-even point each month. If sales are below this number one month, it will usually indicate cash flow problems for the end of the current month and possibly for the next month.

Expanding too quickly without adequate working capital. Many businesses, such as Clara's consulting firm, expand too quickly without adequate working capital. They order inventory without determining the optimum level to maintain, they hire employees without job descriptions and productivity requirements, they spend too much too quickly and borrow without regard to repayment. When sales are plentiful they can cover up all kinds of accounting and cash flow issues. When sales slow down or cash is used up by the expansion the lack of cash flow management and the lack of accounting systems show up and can hurt the company.

Know your break-even point. To manage your business you need to know the sales per month that are required for the business to break-even. To compute this, you need to determine your monthly fixed expenses and the product variable expenses. Your fixed expenses include rent, insurance, bank service charges, utilities, telephone expenses, and basic staffing labor costs. These are essentially the expenses that are due even if no sales are made.

Your variable expenses are those that are incurred when you sell a product. The variable expenses include cost of the product, shipping costs, commissions, referral fees, labor that fluctuates with sales, etc. Variable expenses are normally computed as a percentage of the sales price per unit. The formula for determining break-even for one product line is:

X = Break-even Sales

X – (variable expense percentage times "X") – fixed expenses = zero

Solving the algebra:

X = Fixed expenses divided by (1 – variable expense percentage)

If you have different variable expenses for different product lines, then the formula will be more complicated. An average variable expense can be used to arrive at a target monthly sales figure. Recognize that if you sell more of the more costly product one month, you must also sell more of the less costly product to offset it, or you won't breakeven. I recommend reviewing weekly sales reports and conducting a break-even analysis to anticipate cash flow issues.

Daily expense number. After determining your monthly break-even sales, another number that is useful is your daily expense number. This number is your break-even sales divided by the 30 days or the business days for your business in the month. This represents your target sales each day. These sales numbers must be hit on average to cover the business expenses and must be higher than this to be profitable.

Monthly and annual budgets should be prepared. This is a very important process and should be taken seriously. Start the budget process several months before the year end so that the company's monthly and annual budgets are completed before the New Year starts. See Chapter 2, *Business Plans and Budgets*, for a detailed explanation on the process of developing a budget.

Managers should be involved with preparing their budgets. Managers should either prepare or assist in the preparation of their departments budgets. If they are going to be held accountable for the production or sales of their department then managers need to feel that they own their budget.

Input the monthly budgets into the accounting software. Input the monthly budgets into the accounting software. With the monthly budget in the software, reports can be reviewed during the month and at the end of the month and can actually be compared to the budget.

Monitor weekly financial reports. Preview weekly financial reports comparing the actual income and expenses with the budget. Determine if you are on target and make adjustments as necessary.

Share key numbers with your managers at weekly staff meetings. Your managers are just as responsible for the company success as you are. If they are not aware of their department's successes and failures, they cannot work with you to make adjustments to help the company be more profitable and improve cash flow. Weekly key numbers would include prospect calls, prospect appointments, sales, and aged accounts receivable by customer. The appropriate manager can provide input and accept assignments for follow up and plans of action to improve the various key numbers.

Share monthly financial reports with your managers. Monthly reports that are appropriate for your managers to review include:

1) Actual comparison between the budget and profit center on an accrual basis,
2) Inventory out of stock report,
3) Aged accounts receivable by customer report,
4) Gross profit by product line report,
5) Employee productivity report,
6) Profit and loss report if the managers are responsible for overhead as well.

By including the managers in the reporting and analysis process each month, you can solicit their ideas in managing and reacting to changes in the marketplace and in your business.

Variances in budgets should be explained. The managers and accounting department should research any variances discovered and offer explanations for the differences. If these explanations are appropriate then no action is required.

However, some discrepancies may require corrective action be implemented to correct the result the next month. Both positive and negative variances should be explained. It is important to understand what you are doing right as well as what you should improve.

Budgets may need to be revised during the year. Budgets are tools and are estimates of the future and may or may not predict actual results. If you are aware of changes in the business and company that are definitely changing your prediction for the future, then the budget should be changed. If your budget is approved by a board of directors, you will also need their approval to change it. By changing the budget you can avoid explaining the same variance each month and focus on new variances.

Budget for balance sheet items. Balance sheet items, including accounts receivable, inventory increases, accounts payable, debt decreases, and capital expenditures should be included in the cash flow planning. These items are not on the profit and loss statement and may be overlooked, but they require cash and must be considered to adequately plan for cash needs.

Understand the amount of cash required to run your business. When you plan ahead you can determine the amount of cash required to run your business. At the end of the week you can review the collections expected and payments required to be made the next week and determine any last minute crunches. The last week of the month review the weekly collections expected and the weekly payments projected. This gives you time to plan for any short falls.

Don't assume cash overages are available for withdrawing out of the company. You review a cash flow report and determine that at the end of the month there is $5,000 that appears to be above what is needed for the next month's projected cash needs. Should you withdraw it? Unless you consistently have this overage for several months, I would leave it in the company to be safe.

Invest short-term overages. If you believe that you have a short-term overage, consider transferring this amount to a money market account for a month. If you expect it to be a longer amount of time before you need it, consider paying down your credit line and then possibly purchase a short-term certificate of deposit instead.

Seasonal fluctuations. Some businesses need to save up excess cash in the good months to pay for the slower months and to finance the extra inventory purchases before the seasonal sales begin. As you prepare, your cash flow projections for these short falls and wind falls can help in learning to manage cash better.

Profit does not equal cash. There are timing issues that create differences between the profit indicated on profit and loss statements and the cash in the bank. Just because you had "net income" does not mean that you "made money." Sales are not always collected immediately, they may be charged or billed and take 30 days or more to collect. Vendors may not require you to pay when you place orders and allow you to pay over a period of time. Other timing differences include capital purchases and paying off debt.

Buying capital equipment does not reduce your accounting income and does not necessarily reduce taxable income. Capital expenditures are not usually expensed for accounting purposes when purchased. They are depreciated over a number of years, depending on the type of asset purchased. The cash may be used this month and the expense allocated over a number of months and years. There are tax elections that may allow for some, if not all, of the capital expenditures to be expensed, if you qualify. These are usually available to businesses that do not purchase more than a certain amount of capital items and that make the election on their tax returns. Check with your CPA to see if you qualify for capital expense elections on your tax return.

When should you borrow for capital expenditures? If the monthly income, net of related expenses, exceeds the monthly payment for a capital expenditure, then consider purchasing the item. If the only way that you can afford the capital item is to borrow part of the cost, then borrow the money. Since the company will come out ahead, even though you are borrowing the money, then it is a good business decision to borrow the money. If the capital item will reduce time and employee labor cost or eliminate another expense by more than the monthly payment, it may be a worthwhile debt to incur. However, don't borrow the money for longer than the life of the capital item. Otherwise, when you need to replace the item, you will owe more on the debt than the asset is worth. This happens frequently with vehicles. The car dealers offer extended payment programs and the value of the car decreases faster than the loan does. Just because a loan is offered to you and you qualify for it, doesn't mean you should accept. You have to run the numbers and understand that it makes economic sense to borrow the money under the terms offered.

When is debt ok? Debt is ok when the company can afford to make the payments and still make a profit. Debt is ok if you can expand or grow the company faster with the debt and you can make the payments without straining the company.

Don't use short term financing for a long term asset. If you use a credit line designed to cover cash shortfalls for the purchase of a capital asset that will last longer than a year, the credit line will need to be repaid before the asset is used up. Many long term assets can qualify for collateral and their own loans at lending institutions. Consider these options first.

Establish a credit line with a bank even if you don't need it. Even if you don't believe that you will need a credit line to finance your business, try to establish one anyway. When you don't need it, it is easier to qualify for it and that way, when you need it, you will have it there and available. Unexpected things happen, including unusual expenses, items lost or stolen that have to be replaced immediately to operate the business, unexpected opportunities for sales that require more inventory, or an opportunity to hire an employee earlier than expected.

Paying off debt reduces cash but does not reduce taxable income. Loan payments include both principle and interest payments. The interest is shown on the profit and loss statement as an expense but the principle paid reduces a liability on the balance sheet and is not reflected on the profit and loss statement as an expense.

Income taxes require cash. When you make a profit, you owe income taxes on that profit. The profit that is taxable is taxable income, as computed under the income tax rules. This may be slightly different than the method by which you maintain your books. Consult with your CPA regularly to determine the taxable income and related income taxes that are due. If the partners or shareholders are liable to pay the income taxes, make sure that there is cash available before these payments are due to distribute to them to pay the taxes. If the owner, partner or shareholder is responsible for the income taxes the profit and loss statement will not reflect an income tax expense item. Just because it is not on the profit and loss statement doesn't mean that there are no income taxes due.

Owner, partner and Sub-Chapter S shareholder distributions are balance sheet items. Payments to an owner, a partner and a Sub-Chapter S shareholder above their salary are considered distributions or repayments of existing loans. These payments are not reflected on the profit and loss statement because they are balance sheet items. They still need to be included in the cash flow planning and budgets.

Cash is tied up in your accounts receivable. Sales are the life blood of any business. But sales are not cash until billed and collected. Therefore, managing your accounts receivable system can determine whether you have cash to pay your bills.

Bill often. Your customer is not going to pay you until you present them with a bill. The faster that you send your customers bills or invoices, the faster the terms will start and the faster you will receive the cash.

Prepare bills as often as feasible for the company. Daily billing is preferable because the time between services rendered or the product sale and when the invoice is prepared is minimal. If you wait until the end of the month, the time between the services rendered or sold and the time the invoice is received may be up to 30 days and perhaps 30 more days to pay. This means that it takes 60 days from the sale until cash is received. You can decrease this time by billing sooner and reducing it to a 30 to 35 day turnaround.

Have several ways for your customers to pay. The more ways that your customer can pay you increases the probability of them paying the invoice on time or sooner. Accepting only cash or checks requires the customer to borrow from you if their cash availability is short. If you accept credit cards and checks by phone and can set up or schedule automatic bank drafts, you can accommodate more customers' choice of payment. This allows them to borrow from credit card companies instead of from you.

Eliminate postal mail time. Eliminate postal mail time by emailing invoices and allowing payments to be received online. When you email customers invoices, you eliminate postal mail time. I recommend that you copy your own email address when you send the invoice so that you can verify the invoice was sent. By allowing payments on-line, you speed up the collection process and the wait time for receiving their payment. Make sure that your accounting program allows for these services. If it doesn't, consult with your CPA about programs that will.

Follow up on invoices over credit terms. Set up procedures for following up with customers in the event that the payment due date comes and goes without the payment being received. Customers learn which company's follow-up and which ones don't and they will use this information when cash flow gets tight. Don't let them use you as their bank. The squeaky wheel gets the grease. If you call and bug them they will pay you as soon as they can to get you off their back.

Some banks provide lock boxes. Some banks provide lock boxes for payments received. They open the boxes and deposit the payments into the bank the same day. A report is faxed or emailed to your company on a daily basis to record in your books. This eliminates the time it takes for the staff to open the mail, prepare the deposit, to leave the company premises to go to the bank to make the deposit, and to return to work. It is also more secure because the employees never touch the payments to intercept them or embezzle them, and it allows them to focus on other accounting issues facing the company. However, you must consider the fee the bank charges a fee for this service.

Credit approval procedures. One way to reduce bad debts in the accounts receivable is to establish a credit approval procedure and a process and terms available to each customer. Establish a form for the customer to complete and request business references for a follow-up. Request that they sign a release that can be used to contact the references and obtain credit information. For businesses, you may want to request several years' financial statements which are provided by the businesses' CPA.

Determine the level of credit allowed for each customer and enforce it. After a period of time, during which the customer has paid according to the agreement, increases in the credit limit can be considered. When there are credit problems, a reduction in the credit limit may be appropriate. Manage the credit terms by monitoring the customers' compliance with the credit terms extended by your company.

Accounts receivable factoring. Some companies offer to "buy" your accounts receivable for a reduced price or to loan you a specific amount based on a percentage of the outstanding collectible accounts receivable balance. These companies usually charge a high rate of interest and should be considered only after other financing options have been explored. They provide a rapidly growing company to expand faster than other credit sources would allow.

Cash is tied up in your inventory. If you have inventory on your balance sheet, it has some of your cash tied up in it. The cash invested is the inventory less the balances due in accounts payable for inventory and credit line loans used to purchase inventory. If it is tied up in your inventory, it is not available for other things. Make sure that the amount of cash tied up in your inventory is an appropriate amount based on all of the inventory planning and sales expected and desired inventory levels.

Deferred payment programs for inventory. Some suppliers, especially in anticipation of seasonal orders, will offer special payment terms for purchase of inventory. Instead of the normal 30 day terms, they may offer 60 to 120 day terms. This will allow you time to get into your season and sell some of the items before you have to pay the suppliers. Periodically ask your vendors for special promotional programs so that you can take advantage of these instead of using your valuable bank credit lines.

Floor plans for inventory. Some banks offer loans for floor plans. These loans allow you to purchase larger ticket items that can be specifically identified with identification numbers through a bank loan until sold. You order them and then deliver the invoice to the bank and the bank pays the invoice. As you sell the units, you pay the bank the cost for that unit. Examples of floor plan inventory are cars and boats.

Liquidate inventory when necessary. When cash flow crunches are predicted, plan sales and advertise them ahead of time and mark down merchandise and liquidate inventory. If you have to bill and collect for inventory sales, then you must plan for a longer lead time to turn the sales into cash.

Discounts for paying by a due date. It is important as you manage your business to take advantage of paying invoices to suppliers by the due date for discounts. This may be in 10 days of the date of the invoice or another date. Schedule the due date in the accounting software so that it is not missed if the cash is available to pay it. Some company's record missed discounts as a management expense line item on the profit and loss statement to account for lost opportunities by management.

Set up due dates in accounting software. Schedule all payments due by the company by their due dates and set up alarms for payments so that you don't miss them. Let your computer do the work. I recommend filing unpaid invoices in alphabetical order in a pending accounts payable file. If you file by due date and you receive additional correspondence, you have to spend time going through all slots to match up invoices by company. The computer will keep track of the due date and track the pending file by company name.

Allow for mail time. Don't put the due date in the accounting software that is the due date that the payment must be received by the supplier or creditor. Take the due date and subtract mail time, usually three to five business days, as well as the time for printing, reviewing, signing, and stuffing which may be an additional two to three business days. Enter this date in the computer.

Avoid penalties and late fees. By monitoring the due dates and cash flow required to meet your payment obligations, you should be able to avoid penalties and late fees. This can add up when you have cash flow problems.

Set up a schedule for printing checks. Set up a schedule for printing checks. I recommend picking a day of the week to print checks. Monday print the payments due that week for review by the owner. The owner approves some or all of the payments, the checks are printed on Wednesday, and then the owner reviews and signs the checks by Thursday. On Friday, the checks are stuffed in the envelopes and mailed.

Weekly reports for bills due. Weekly reports for bills due should be generated for review by the owner and approval for payment. If cash is tight that week, the owner has to decide where to obtain the cash to pay the bills or delay paying the bills.

Credit card financing. Corporate credit cards can be used for employee expenses to prevent the employee having to use their personal cards. It is important that you have all employees with access to the corporate credit cards sign a statement that they understand that the card is to be used only for corporate business and if they leave the company and there are any personal charges on the credit card these charges are to be repaid immediately. If not repaid immediately, they will be deducted from the employee's last check and any remaining balance will be due to the company under specified terms. Even an employee having access to an owner's credit card to assist with ordering and charging goods and services needs to sign statement as indicated above.

Employee credit cards. Some companies require that employees use their own credit cards to pay for business expenses and then submit an expense report for reimbursement before the credit card payment is due. The company is not directly liable for any charges on the card, but since it's his card, the employee is. So if personal charges appear on the card the company doesn't have to worry about paying them.

Be careful using credit cards for financing business expenditures for more than a month. As long as these are charges are paid off monthly, then the use of the credit cards is appropriate. If companies use cash advances from credit cards to finance short term cash shortfalls in the company or they charge capital expenditures that aren't paid off that month, then the credit from the credit cards may not be used appropriately. Clara fell into this trap of using credit cards and not managing the debt. See Chapter 7, *Raising Capital*, for other items regarding credit cards.

Owners can be a source of cash. Owners may be able to loan the company cash in shortfalls. The owners need to be made aware of the anticipated shortfalls so that they can transfer funds or liquidate assets as necessary.

Payroll expenses. Payroll expenses after inventory may be your largest monthly expenditure. The longer you can wait to pay employees the longer you have to collect cash from the sales from your customers. Unfortunately, employees will only wait so long, as they have bills to pay as well. I recommend paying twice a month, the fifteenth and the last day of the month. This keeps the monthly expenses captured within the same month and no accruals are necessary and twice a month is usually the fewest number of times that you can pay employees in a month and stay competitive as an employer.

Lay off employees when necessary. Review employee productivity reports and if the employee is not producing nor trying to improve, lay them off. Use the payroll labor dollars for employees who are producing. Clara may have to lay off an employee or two until she gets her company back on its cash flow feet.

Reduce expenses. Periodically review your company expenses and reduce them when appropriate. You can reduce expenses to a certain level, at which you compromise the quality of the goods and services offered by your company. Don't count the paper clips. I attended a seminar in my early business life and the instructor jumped up on the table and yelled "don't count the paperclips". He explained that you can spend time analyzing and counting every expense item over and over and it will only save you so much money. The real secret to making more money is to concentrate on the top line, sales, and work on ways to increase them. This is a better use of your time if you want to make more money.

Frequent flyer miles and other discount and rebate programs. Another way to reduce expenses is to take advantage of frequent flyer miles against plane fare costs, gas cards and other point programs that can be exchanged for merchandise and goods and services. The company can utilize these without spending more money. Review credit card offers periodically and make sure that you are using the cards that are providing the benefits and programs that you want and that you receive the most benefits.

Barter companies. Barter companies offer the opportunity to trade for goods and services and not exchange cash. If the barter company has goods and services that you will use and they have other members who will use your goods and services, then it may be appropriate to participate in their programs. The sales that are "sold" through this program are still recorded as income and sales tax is still due when appropriate and goods "purchased" are deductions in the company or will also be income to you if it is used personally. This requires careful accounting, as no cash is exchanged. If it is rare that the amount sold equals the amount purchased, so the balance is recorded as either an asset or a liability. Be careful that you don't record a large number of credits from members using your services if you don't have ways to benefit from these credits.

Difference between a want and a need. A need is something that is basic and required to run your business. A want is something above and beyond the basic and required needs of the company. Buying a stapler that staples is a need. Buying a stapler that is electric and has extra features that are not required by the company is a want. Sometimes wants can be indulged by the company but cash flow and profitability will dictate the ability to splurge on these items.

Critique every expenditure. Evaluate whether you really need the item that you are considering purchasing. Determine the required features. Decide whether it is a want or a need and whether the company can afford it.

Small items add up. The stapler example may seem small and inconsequential but it is the mindset, more so than the dollar amount, that is important. Small items have a way of adding up and having an impact on the bottom line and cash flow. So these need to be monitored as well.

Employees will spend more if you spend more. The old saying "do as I say not as I do" is hard to enforce in a business. Leadership starts at the top. If you are extravagant and wasteful, the employees will tend to be too. They will justify their expenses and find ways to exploit the system. Set the example and your employees will respect you and follow suit with a little prodding from you.

Plan to reinvest in your company. Some owners take every extra dime out of the company. If you want to have less stress in managing the cash flow of your business and you want to grow your business responsibly, consider reinvesting or leaving in your company a certain percentage of profits. Consider 25 to 50% of profits for income taxes depending on tax brackets, 20 to 50% profit withdrawal depending on the tax burden and 20 to 25% reinvestment in your company. Some companies share the profits with the employees as profit sharing bonuses. Establish a plan and stick to it.

Determine working capital that is required. By planning with a budget and considering both the balance sheet items and profit and loss statement requirements for cash each month, a working capital threshold amount should be established. It is important to establish a goal of having working capital on hand at any given moment to meet three months of cash payment requirements in case there are no sales. This is usually referred to the working capital of the company. This goal provides for flexibility with cash requirements each week.

Save for large expenditures. Instead of counting on credit to purchase large expenditures, consider saving the money before you purchase it. If the need for the item is not immediate and you can plan ahead, part of the monthly excess cash received can be ear-marked for this expenditure.

Extraordinary things happen. No matter how hard you plan, extraordinary things happen and usually when you least expect them. Therefore it is important to budget for an un-budgeted item or event and be prepared for when it happens. Extraordinary items include large repairs and maintenance, requirements to move by landlord, and theft or loss of equipment or inventory.

Establish a relationship with a banker. It is so very important to establish a relationship with a banker. Keep the banker informed as to your business financial situation and obtain pre-approval for credit lines and loans. Always give your banker an opportunity to loan you money before you go shopping. If you banker is more competitive than the financing available through other sources, then accept their loan. Sometimes the banker rates can be used to negotiate better rates with the other companies offering the credit for the purchase. Always give the banker the opportunity to match the terms. Many banks have a maximum amount of credit that is allowable per company. They have a variety of formulas that are used. There may be a maximum period even on the best company balance sheet, and there may be a maximum based on the assets of the company and the debt to asset ratio or other key ratios. Make sure that you are aware of these maximums set by the bank. You may want to use the outside financing and leave the bank credit available for other purchases or cash needs.

Communicate with your creditors. When you get into cash flow trouble, communicate with your creditors. Sometimes they will offer extended payment terms or forgive or defer a payment. Clara needs to contact her creditors and see what options she has to work out the repayment of the debt.

Debt counselors. When you get into trouble, there are debt counselors that are available to consult with you and assist you in getting back on your feet. These services range from telling you what to do to taking over the managing of the debt and communication with the creditors. The fees vary with the level of service. Some companies set up payment plans with the creditors and you send them one or two checks a month and they distribute them accordingly.

SBA services and loans. The Small Business Administration has Small Business Development Centers around the country that have counselors on staff and volunteers who are available to assist you with developing budgets and systems to manage your cash flow. Many of these services are free and others have low fees depending on the work involved. They can also recommend banks that work with the SBA and offer SBA guaranteed loans. See Chapter 7, *Raising Capital*, for more information.

Managing cash flow is your most critical responsibility as an owner. Your customers, your vendors, your creditors and your employees depend upon you to do a good job of managing your cash flow. The entire success of your company is dependent on your ability to manage your cash flow successfully. Please take this responsibility seriously and ask for assistance when you need help.

MANAGING CASH FLOW CHECKLIST

	Strategy	Page Ref #	Application To Your Business
1.	Know where you stand at all times	145	
2.	Bank balance is not your book cash balance	145	
3.	Anticipate cash flow problems	146	
4.	Expanding too quickly without adequate working capital	146	
5.	Know your breakeven point	146	
6.	Daily expense number	147	
7.	Monthly and annual budgets should be prepared	147	
8.	Managers should be involved with preparing their budgets	147	
9.	Input the monthly budgets into the accounting software	147	
10.	Monitor weekly financial reports	148	
11.	Share key numbers with your managers at weekly staff meetings	148	
12.	Share monthly financial reports with your managers	148	

	Strategy	Page Ref #	Application To Your Business
13.	Variances in budgets should be explained	148	
14.	Budgets may need to be revised during the year	149	
15.	Budget for balance sheet items	149	
16.	Understand the amount of cash required to run your business	149	
17.	Don't assume cash overages are available for withdrawing out of the company	149	
18.	Invest short-term overages	149	
19.	Seasonal fluctuations	150	
20.	Profit does not equal cash	150	
21.	Buying capital equipment does not reduce your accounting income and does not necessarily reduce taxable income	150	
22.	When should you borrow for capital expenditures?	150	
23.	When is debt ok?	151	
24.	Don't use short term financing for a long term asset	151	

	Strategy	Page Ref #	Application To Your Business
25.	Establish a credit line with a bank even if you don't need it	151	
26.	Paying off debt reduces cash but does not reduce taxable income	151	
27.	Income taxes require cash	151	
28.	Owner, partner and Sub-Chapter S shareholder distributions are balance sheet items	152	
29.	Cash is tied up in your accounts receivable	152	
30.	Bill often	152	
31.	Have several ways for your customers to pay	152	
32.	Eliminate postal mail time	153	
33.	Follow up on invoices over credit terms	153	
34.	Some banks provide lock boxes	153	
35.	Credit approval procedures	153	
36.	Accounts receivable factoring	154	
37.	Cash is tied up in your inventory	154	

	Strategy	Page Ref #	Application To Your Business
38.	Deferred payment programs for inventory	154	
39.	Floor plans for inventory	154	
40.	Liquidate inventory when necessary	154	
41.	Discounts for paying by a due date	155	
42.	Set up due dates in accounting software	155	
43.	Allow for mail time	155	
44.	Avoid penalties and late fees	155	
45.	Set up a schedule for printing checks	155	
46.	Weekly reports for bills due	155	
47.	Credit card financing	156	
48.	Employee credit cards	156	
49.	Owners can be a source of cash	156	
50.	Payroll expenses	156	
51.	Lay off employees when necessary	157	
52.	Reduce expenses	157	
53.	Frequent flyer miles and other discount and rebate programs	157	

	Strategy	Page Ref #	Application To Your Business
54.	Barter companies	157	
55.	Difference between a want and a need	158	
56.	Critique every expenditure	158	
57.	Small items add up	158	
58.	Employees will spend more if you spend more	158	
59.	Plan to reinvest in your company	158	
60.	Determine Working capital that is required	158	
61.	Save for large expenditures	159	
62.	Extraordinary items happen	159	
63.	Establish a relationship with a banker	159	
64.	Communicate with your creditors	159	
65.	Debt counselors	160	
66.	SBA services and loans	160	
67.	Managing cash flow is your most critical responsibility as an owner	160	

CHAPTER 15
Inventory

Aline has a furniture store and inventory is the biggest asset on her balance sheet. Some items she can't keep in stock and some items she can't seem to sell. She noticed that the inventory was increasing and the sales were stagnant and she was concerned. She needed a system to manage her inventory.

Too much cash tied up in inventory. You may have heard of being house poor after you purchase a new home, when your balance sheet looks great with this new asset but you don't have any cash in the bank. Well you can be inventory poor in your business as well, with great looking assets recorded on your books, but no cash in the bank. Inventory is an asset that can feel like a liability when too much cash is tied up in it.

System to manage your inventory. Most small businesses don't have a reliable method of managing their inventory. Some owners walk around their store and write down items to reorder and if they see items that have been sitting there awhile, they mark them down or move them to a sale area. This may work for really small stores, but as you grow, one person will not be able to manage it as efficiently as necessary. Develop a reliable system to manage your inventory; don't let your inventory manage you.

Inventory software programs can help. I recommend accounting programs that include an inventory module. When you make entries into the inventory section, they are automatically entered into the accounting section as well. I don't recommend utilizing a stand alone inventory software program that does not communicate with and download information to your accounting program. Reports must be printed off the stand alone inventory program and then re-keyed into the accounting program, thus errors can occur. If you have two systems that don't agree, which one is correct? This situation requires more hours to reconcile the problem, and those hours could be better spent managing your business.

Know your customer. Some business owners start out buying inventory from their own perspective as a consumer. They find that their customers buy some of this inventory and some of it just sits on the shelf. By learning what products your customers are buying you can reorder these items and look for similar items to purchase. How can you learn more about your customer? In your software program, print a report that indicates inventory sales by product and inventory turnover numbers by product. By reviewing this report on at least a monthly basis, you can then adjust your inventory purchases in accordance with this information. Take these reports to the Mart with you as well, so that you don't rely on your memory when making purchases.

Just because you like the product doesn't mean that your customers will purchase it. Consider the process of learning what your customers want to purchase as an experiment. Sometimes it is trial and error so purchase an item and see if it sells in a prescribed period of time. Move it around the store and then reduce the price until it sells. If it takes longer than normal to sell buy something else. By knowing your customer, you can keep from purchasing more items that won't sell and increasing your inventory investment more than necessary.

Visit the Industry Marts with an open mind. Visit the Industry Marts with an open mind. Ask the Mart personnel about trends that they are seeing in the marketplace and what things should you be considering for this next season. They keep their finger on the pulse of the marketplace, including your competitors, and they are an excellent resource for information.

Hard to sell something that you don't have. It is hard to sell something that you don't have in the store. If a customer is looking for a specific item they may ask a store clerk if you can order what they need. Generally, if the customer doesn't see it, they don't think about buying it. After learning how many items you sell each year of a product, you can better plan to determine how many you need to keep in stock. You are trying to accomplish a number of goals at one time, by having the least amount of investment in the inventory while having the product available when your customer wants to purchase it.

Turnover rate. The turnover rate is the number of times that your inventory has "turned" to generate the income during a year period. It is computed by dividing your annual sales by the average balance in your inventory. The general rule is the higher the number is the better. You want to determine the least amount of inventory that you need to maintain at any given point to generate the targeted sales. The lower the inventory required to generate the desired sales, the less space required and less investment required to maintain the inventory. There are websites that list inventory turnover rates by Standard Industry Codes (SIC). These are important to use as guidelines, even though your local area or niche in the industry may require slightly different rates than the industry as a whole. As you review your inventory reports and notice low turnover rates on specific products, you may want to reduce the number on hand or make them special order only.

Move slow moving items. As you review your inventory reports, don't be afraid to reduce prices on slow moving items and sell them. If customers who frequent your store see the same old things all the time, they will not come as often. Reduce items that have not been sold in 30 days and then reduce again in another 30 days and keep them moving. This will free up inventory dollars to replace them with products that your customers want to purchase at regular price.

Reorder quantity and reorder point. If you sell an average of 10 items of a product per month and it takes two weeks to a month to receive items after ordering, then you need to order at least 10 per month. Called the "reorder point", you restock when you have 11 units of this product on hand. This allows an extra one to be on the shelf, just in case more customers want this item. If you can order today and have it delivered tomorrow, you can order fewer items at a time. As your sales increase, the quantity to order and the reorder point may need to be adjusted.

Seasonal fluctuations. Some businesses have seasonal fluctuations and must increase their inventory to prepare for the increases and then decrease in the slower times. The Holidays are example of increasing inventory in the fall to allow customers to purchase more items for Holiday presents. Clothes and equipment sold at ski resorts have a limited sales season — as long as there is snow on the ground they're in season. Inventory has to be ordered prior to these seasons and be available when the customers need and want to buy it. Then, toward the end of the season, it needs to be marked down and liquidated to prevent storing and holding until next season.

Review out of stock items. In theory, if the re-order points are accurate, you should never be out of stock of any item. Review this report each month and research the reasons for having certain items out of stock. Certain suppliers may be taking longer to fill their orders and the re-order point may need to be adjusted. You may have changed suppliers and their time between order and delivery is longer than the old supplier. It may be a one time situation, due to a strike or weather issue and should be monitored temporarily.

You may need to raise your prices. If you have access to an unlimited supply of a particular product and can order and receive them quickly, the price may be fine. If you can't keep an item in stock, you may need to raise the price of the product. If you have a limited number of items of a product to sell, the price needs to reflect the limited availability. General Motors limits the number of Corvettes that it manufactures per year, particularly on special editions. It is not uncommon for customers to pay above list price to be one of the few customers each year that are able to buy a special edition Corvette.

Special and custom orders. Customers may request that you special order items that you don't normally stock or that you have custom orders made to their specifications. Aline in her furniture store may have books for customers to review to order other colors or other styles of furniture. She may also have fabric books for the customer to select a fabric to cover a particular sofa or chair. On special orders that can be returned to the supplier, I recommend that a deposit equal to your cost including shipping to and from be collected from the customer. If a restocking fee is charged by the supplier in the event the item has to be returned, then that cost should be included in the deposit as well. Then, if the customer never picks the item up or changes their mind, you are not out any money. If it is a custom order that has limited to no interest to other customers, it is a good idea to require 100% of the sales price as a deposit before ordering the item.

Protect your inventory. Since inventory is the major asset on your balance sheet and selling it makes money for your company; you need to protect it from both customers and employees. Shelves in the store should be low enough to see over the top and monitor your customers' activities. If the products have large per unit prices and are easy to put in customer's pockets, such as jewelry, they should be displayed in locked glass cases to prevent shoplifting. Trusted employees can be authorized to show these products to customers. Rules can be established and communicated to your employees. An employee should only work with one customer and only have one item out of the case at a time and the case should be re-closed after removing or returning each item. It is also a good idea to require that another employee or even a manager check out another employee's purchase.

Electronic inventory tags. Electronic inventory tags can be attached to each product and electronic gates at the entrances and exits of the store can be installed. When a customer purchases the product, the inventory tag is removed or deactivated so that the customer can leave the store without setting off the alarms. If someone tries to leave the store without purchasing the product, the alarms will be activated and the clerks can ask for the product to be returned, or the store can press formal shoplifting charges. The electronic tags can allow the store clerks to concentrate on selling the products and servicing the customers instead of being the inventory protectors.

Consider having a gate at the employee entrance as well, so that employees are not tempted to slip out with inventory under their clothes or coats. Many retail stores have standing policies for a manager to check employees' bags or purses before they leave the premises each time. This practice is most effective in stores where inventory is kept in bottles, small boxes, or other easily portable containers.

Electronic security systems can be installed. A security system that has cameras around the store and a store clerk or security guard that monitors the customers' activities is a useful measure that many companies implement for inventory control. Consider installing an electronic security system that has door and window monitors and motion detectors. If these are triggered and the alarm is not deactivated within a few minutes, an alarm is sent to the local police department for immediate investigation. Sometimes the landlord may be willing to install and include such a system in the price of the rent and this possibility should be discussed when negotiating the lease. See Chapter 6, *Choosing Your Business Location*, for more points in negotiating your lease.

Night security guards. Some shopping centers have nighttime security guards that patrol the parking lots and back entrances of stores in the center. If you do not have this included in your lease or complex, you may want to contact local security companies. They may be able to add you to a driving circuit that already exits, in which they visit your store location several times a night and patrol the parking lot and back entrance and check the doors. You can then post a sign that states that this security company patrols your premises at night.

Insurance coverage. Discuss with your insurance agent the ways to protect your inventory. By having an alarm system, security patrols, and inventory tags, your insurance costs may be reduced. Make sure that your agent understands your inventory and that if it is stolen or destroyed, it will be replaced with the least amount of effort and documentation, so that you can be up and selling again as soon as possible. It's important that this is replacement cost insurance so that you have the dollars to replace the inventory that was stolen or damaged. If you have regular insurance and the insurance company depreciates the existing inventory or fixtures, you will not receive the dollars you need to replace the inventory and fixtures. While every business owner hopes they'll never need to file a claim with their insurance company, if it becomes necessary, they need to have the correct coverage. So take the time to work with your agent and ask lots of questions until you understand the options and the various types of insurance coverage available.

Know the cost of your inventory. No one outside your company is going to track the cost of your inventory. You must take responsibility for knowing the cost of your inventory. If you sell a product below your cost or with a marginal profit by mistake, it is no one's fault but your own. As you monitor all of the costs that are incurred in your inventory from ordering, delivering, stocking, selling, shipping, you will need to adjust the sales price of your product. Sometimes these costs and the necessary related price changes will involve increases and sometimes decreases. The more aware you are of these costs, the more competitive you can be in the marketplace by keeping your prices up-to-date. This knowledge is powerful in the business world.

Carrying and storing costs. Carrying inventory and displaying it on the shelf in your store costs you money. The floor space per square foot needs to be computed. The rent, utilities and costs associated with the inventory, such as the interest on loans, security, and insurance costs should be totaled and divided by the floor space available for the inventory. The rest of the floor space should not be included, as it is used by the service personnel in the business of selling the inventory. This per-square-foot-of-inventory-floor-space cost is important to know and to allocate to each product to determine the carrying cost for each item. If it takes two months to sell a product sitting on the shelf, then two months of carrying cost should be considered as part of the cost of the product and the price should be adjusted accordingly. If the price cannot be increased to cover the carrying cost, then you may need to consider discontinuing that product. If the products are ordered for a large promotion or seasonal fluctuation and they have to be stored, this storage cost must be included in the carrying and storing costs.

Shipping costs. Suppliers typically add shipping costs to the price of an order. They usually have a specific shipping company that they have negotiated special rates to ship their products. If the company contracts for the shipping, you do not actually own the product until you accept delivery of it. If it is damaged en route, the supplier may have a claim against the shipping company.

Stocking and re-stocking labor costs. Once the product is delivered, it must be unpacked, recorded as received, and put on the shelves or display units. This requires employee time and labor costs. When customers pick up products and leave them around the store without purchasing them, they have to be re-stocked by employees. When customers return items that are not damaged, either gifts or items they changed their mind about, these products have to be re-stocked by employees as well. When these items are waiting to be re-stocked, they are not available for new customers to see and purchase, thus sales might be lost. So employees must be trained and available to re-stock during the day to keep the inventory in front of the customers. Some companies have crews that come in the evening when the store is closed and unpack and stock at night. All of these labor costs must be considered in the cost of the product as well.

Re-stocking fee. Some companies charge a re-stocking fee when an item is returned to the company. Usually these are larger ticket items or special order items. Regular retail operations that are competing for customers generally don't charge this fee.

Selling costs. Once the product is ordered, delivered and stocked on the shelf, it still has to be sold. The employees answer questions and suggest ways that the customer may be able to use the product or suggest other reasons for purchasing it. These employees are selling the product and their labor costs are included in the selling cost. Other selling costs include cost of displays, video or audio programs, commissions or incentives to employees, referral fees to customers, and rebates. These also need to be recorded and considered in the cost of the products.

Loss leaders. Some companies carry products that actually lose them money. Their plan is to bring customers into the store that will want to buy these special priced products and hope that they buy other profitable products. Monitor these loss leaders carefully and make sure that they are doing what you need them to do. Any business owner would prefer to break-even instead of losing money on these products, if possible.

Provide Samples. Food courts and grocery stores sometimes will have samples of their foods or dishes available for the customer to try before they purchase. Perfume is another example of a customer needing to try before purchasing. Furniture stores such as Aline's should have furniture available to try out, to feel the texture of the fabric, to sit on, and lie down on. Electronic stores with gadgets have some on display for customers to turn on and see what they do. Consider ways that your customers can experience your products that will help make them want to purchase from you.

Short shelf life. Some products, such as fresh food, have a short period of time during which they can be sold. The expiration dates need to be monitored very carefully. Knowing when you need to re-order and how many you normally sell during a given period of time is even more critical for this type of product than for non-perishables. If you make a mistake and order too much, you can't just leave it on the shelf until it sells, you have to throw it away, which gets very expensive.

You also have to have a system of monitoring the expiration dates and removing them from the shelf as soon as they are expired. Customers are not happy when they notice that you are attempting to sell expired products, whether intentionally or not. You can assign the job of physically looking at the products on the shelf every day or every other day to an employee. If your inventory program has a field to record this information, you can run reports daily to show you which products should be removed from the shelves. Adjust re-order points and quantities if you are consistently throwing away products above acceptable levels.

Presentation is key. Customers have to notice your product in the store and understand its use and then want to purchase it before a sale happens. If the products are jammed in together and the customer has to pull them apart and do work to see what is on the shelf, the products are not going to be seen by everyone and will not sell as quickly. Orderly shelves and displays are eye-pleasing and more likely to draw the attention of a customer. If you can display a product in use or with a video describing its uses, the customer is more likely to stop and consider this product.

Floor plan of store. The floor plan should make it easy for the customer to find the products that they are looking for. Book stores usually organize their books alphabetical by author, title, or subject. Aline's furniture store could be organized by rooms of the house. The living room area could have sofas, easy chairs, end tables, and lamps or other accessories. Having charts or lists at the end of each aisle with the types of products on that aisle is helpful for the customer. If you have more than one store, providing similar floor plans for the same named store will provide customers the comfort that they can go into any of your stores and not have to start from scratch to find something.

Don't put the petite clothing on the top rack. It is important to think of the demographics of the customer that may be purchasing a particular product. Petite customers are generally shorter than the average population and have a difficult time reaching the top shelf for clothing. If you put their clothes on these racks they probably will not see the clothes and become too frustrated. They may ask for help, once, but they will try and find a more user-friendly store the next time.

Clean store. A dirty store gives the impression that the owner does not care enough about it to keep it clean. Do they care about the inventory and is it maintained and looked after even though the store is not? People may feel uncomfortable and feel dirty too and then not stay in the store very long. You want customers to have a positive shopping experience and you should take away any barriers for them to do business with you. Hire a maintenance person to come into the store every night to clean the floor and dust the shelves and clean the bathrooms. It will make a major difference to your customers and potential customers.

Use the Internet to sell your products. Many companies have physical store locations and also offer their products via the Internet. This is a way of expanding your store without having to incur all of the store location and personnel expenses. See Chapter 12, *Internet Marketing and Websites*, for more information.

May have to use the accrual method of accounting. If a significant amount of your income is generated from inventory sales, depending on your annual sales and your entity type, you may be required to use the accrual method of accounting when you report your taxable income to the IRS. Check with your CPA to determine what method you are required to use. I recommend the accrual method for accounting and managing your business in most cases. Your income is recorded when you as the seller have done everything required to complete the sale on your end, including shipping or delivery to the buyer. The income may be booked as a receivable and you may have to wait to collect the cash. The expenses are recorded when incurred by the company and not when paid. This method provides you as the business owner the best indication of the performance of your business in a particular month. If you only look at the cash balance, you can be deceived and think that you are doing better or worse than you are.

Inventory is not an expense until sold. When inventory is purchased it is recorded as an asset. Then, when it is sold, the cost is withdrawn from inventory and recorded as a cost of sale expense or cost of goods sold expense. Some companies expense all inventory purchases in their accounting system as cost of goods sold and then once a year they adjust for the ending inventory balance. This method records the appropriate gross profit and profitability annually, but not monthly. I recommend the former method if at all possible so that you can manage your inventory and your business more profitably, and you can identify any problems in profitability early on.

Buying inventory does not reduce taxable income. Inventory is an asset and spending cash on buying products uses up cash in the bank but does not reduce your profit or net taxable income. Over and over again clients have told me, "What do you mean I owe taxes, I don't have any cash in the bank." Be careful and work with you CPA to know your estimated tax liability and set aside the cash for taxes so that you are not surprised.

Gross profit percentage should be monitored. The sales price minus the cost of goods sold is the gross profit. The gross profit divided by the sales price is the gross profit percentage and this is the percentage that you have generated from each sales dollar to cover the overhead and your profit. Each product and product line may have different gross profit percentages and may need to be reviewed separately. The company gross profit percentage is a blended rate from all sales and all product lines. As you review these reports monthly, prices may need to be increased when this percentage begins to decrease.

Deferred payment programs and floor plans. Some suppliers, especially in anticipation of seasonal orders, will offer special payment terms. See Chapter 14, *Managing Cash Flow*, for more details.

Year-end inventory may be taxed by local authorities. Some cities or counties or states may assess a tax on the value of your year end inventory for doing business in their area. Check with your CPA to determine if you are subject to a tax. If you are, you may want to plan sales and inventory reduction sales before your year end to have your inventory as low as possible. You may want to schedule deliveries for new orders for after the year-end as well.

Review, monitor, and manage your inventory. To both improve your bottom line and keep the minimal investment in inventory required to run your business as profitably as possible, you need to develop, review, and monitor systems to manage your inventory.

INVENTORY CHECKLIST

	Strategy	Page Ref #	Application To Your Business
1.	Too much cash tied up in inventory	167	
2.	System to manage your inventory balance	167	
3.	Inventory software programs can help	167	
4.	Know your customer	168	
5.	Visit the Industry Marts with an open mind	168	
6.	Hard to sell something that you don't have	168	
7.	Turnover rate	169	
8.	Move slow moving items	169	
9.	Reorder quantity and reorder point	169	
10.	Seasonal fluctuations	169	
11.	Review out of stock items	170	
12.	You may need to raise your prices	170	
13.	Special and custom orders	170	
14.	Protect your inventory	171	

	Strategy	Page Ref #	Application To Your Business
15.	Electronic inventory tags	171	
16.	Electronic security systems can be installed	171	
17.	Night security guards	172	
18.	Insurance coverage	172	
19.	Know the cost of your inventory	172	
20.	Carrying and storing costs	173	
21.	Shipping costs	173	
22.	Stocking and re-stocking labor costs	173	
23.	Re-stocking fee	174	
24.	Selling costs	174	
25.	Loss leaders	174	
26.	Provide Samples	174	
27.	Short shelf life	174	
28.	Presentation is key	175	
29.	Floor plan of store	175	
30.	Don't put the petite clothing on the top rack	175	

	Strategy	Page Ref #	Application To Your Business
31.	Clean store	176	
32.	Use the Internet to sell your products	176	
33.	May have to use the accrual method of accounting	176	
34.	Inventory is not an expense until sold	177	
35.	Buying inventory does not reduce taxable income	177	
36.	Gross profit percentage should be monitored	177	
37.	Deferred payment programs and floor plans	177	
38.	Year-end inventory may be taxed by local authorities	177	
39.	Review, monitor, and manage your inventory	178	

CHAPTER 16
Buying Versus Leasing

Lee leased a car for five years and recorded the lease in his business name. He used the car 75% for business and drove an average of 15,000 miles per year. The lease provided an additional charge for miles in excess of the first 12,000 per year. He found out that he was incurring repairs every month and decided that he wanted to terminate the lease at the end of three years and purchase or lease another car. He discovered that he owed hundreds of dollars in excessive mileage charges and that he had to buy out the balance of the lease payments. There was not a discount or the ability to pay off only the principle balance. Should Lee have leased or purchased this car?

I am frequently asked these questions. Should I lease or buy a car, and should it be in the name of the business?

Title the car in business if use more than 50% for business use. It doesn't matter whether the car is in the business name or titled personally, only the cost of the business use can be taken as a business deduction. I usually recommend that if the car is used for more than 50% for business, then putting it in the name of the business makes sense. The actual cost of the personal use of the car is income to the owner. If it is used for less than 50% than it probably makes sense to have it outside the business and bill the business the mileage rate for the business use. Remember that commuting to and from the home to the office is not business use.

Since Lee uses his car 75% for business, I would recommend that it be titled in the business name.

Purchase the car whenever possible. Should he lease or purchase? There are several issues with leasing that most people do not consider. When you lease a car you are paying someone else to purchase the vehicle, borrow the money, and to make a profit on your lease. Therefore, if you can borrow the money, you can eliminate paying someone else that profit on the lease. Many times the first and last lease payments and the security deposit would provide a down payment on a purchase. Then that extra profit is cut out and saved by the business owner.

Leasing causes a liability and no asset on the balance sheet. With a lease, you have a liability on your balance sheet and no asset as the leased vehicle usually remains titled in the leasor's name. When you purchase the car it becomes an asset on your balance sheet and the loan is recorded as an offsetting liability.

No residual value when lease is terminated. When the loan is paid off you still have the residual value of the car which may be realized by selling it. In a lease, you have nothing to show for paying all of the payments. Even if you sell the car before the loan is paid off, there is still residual value to offset the principle loan balance. Lee also realized that he had no residual value in the car to sell. If he owned the car, the car would be worth something to offset the liability due. Sometimes if the loan is long enough, the value is not worth as much as the liability, but it is still better than no value.

Must pay balance of lease payments if terminate early. In a purchase the principle is due to be paid off, not the balance of note payments including interest. When you want to pay off a lease you pay an amount equal to all of the remaining payments. Lee discovered that terminating the lease early, he was still liable to pay off the entire balance of the lease payments. If he had purchased it and wanted to sell it, he would only have to payoff the principle of the loan.

Headaches of ownership without the rights. In leasing, you have all of the headaches of ownership without the rights. If your leased car breaks down you have to pay to fix it, just as if you own it. If the lessor provided you with a loaner while your leased vehicle was being fixed at no charge, then maybe it might make a difference. Some dealerships provide loaner cars during the warranty period when you purchase the car. With leasing, you still have to pay for the tag and related annual state taxes and pay for the annual insurance costs.

May have to pay sales tax on the interest. Many states charge sales tax on the entire lease payment, so the 'interest' is taxed as well. When you purchase a car, most states tax the purchase price of the car and some states subtract the value of the trade in before sales tax is computed. Purchasing definitely saves sales tax and in some states that can add up.

Mileage overages are expensive on leases. Lease payments are determined based on a certain annual mileage usage. There are substantial charges for mileage overages on leases. When you own your car the value of the car is reduced for excessive mileage, but this is usually less than the lease overage charges. Lee also should have noted the mileage use rate at 12,000 mile per year and if he still decided to lease, should have negotiated a lease payment with the 15,000 miles per year at a reasonable rate. The leasing company really makes money on overages.

Sometimes it is "OK" to lease. When is it 'OK' to lease? If you only need a car temporarily or you don't know what kind of car you want, a short term lease may make sense. Sometimes, there are leasing specials for short term leases, with no money down and reasonable monthly lease payments, these may make sense for the short term. If you do not have any credit available to purchase and need assets for your business to operate, then leasing may be an option to obtain the assets and start making money on them now.

When a leased car is totaled, the balance of lease payments are still due to be paid. If you are in an accident in a leased car and it is totaled. The balance of lease payments is still due to the lessor, and the insurance company is only going to pay the current fair value of the car. You are responsible for the balance due to the leasing company. Some leasing companies offer insurance protection for this deficit, but it costs more money and increases your lease payment. Evaluate the cost and the benefit.

Negotiate the best cash deal first. If you are negotiating with a dealership, always negotiate for the best cash deal, then, bring up the financing option and then the lease deal. With the Internet you can research the value of your car if you are trading it in, and the value of the car that you want and go into the dealership armed with this information. Check with your bank for financing rates before visiting the dealership. The salesperson and dealership both make money on the financing and the leasing, and you want to pay the least amount possible.

Be prepared to walk out of the dealership and to double check numbers. It is all about numbers, it is ok to walk out of the dealership and use your computer to double check the numbers. I once negotiated for the purchase of a car and they told me that they were giving me a certain interest rate and things just didn't add up. So I left the dealership and used my office computer to determine the interest rate based on the deal that they gave me and the interest rate that they were charging me was 3% higher than what they quoted. I called and they apologized and corrected the numbers before I would purchase the car. There are many honest dealerships with which to do business, but sometimes they are hard to find. Do your research and keep all of them honest. The best day to purchase a car is the last day of the month or quarter. They are trying to make their quotas and are sometimes willing to make better deals.

May consider leasing phone systems, furniture and computer systems. Other assets that may be needed for your business that you will need to determine whether to buy or to lease include: phone systems, furniture and computer systems. The same considerations listed above for whether to purchase or lease a car should be applied to these decisions as well.

Phone systems should have features that will save time and allow your employees to be efficient. Phone systems are necessary equipment for a business. A voice mail system should also be included. If you are a one-person shop, an answering machine and a single phone with one or two lines may be adequate. As you expand and hire employees a phone system with voice mail is important. Employees need to be able to retrieve messages remotely and transfer messages to one another. Sometimes companies have refurbished equipment for half the new cost and this equipment is just as good as new. Ask about them, and check the paper for businesses upgrading phone systems or moving. I sold my system for twice what the company offered me in trade-in and the guy who purchased my system still bought it at half the retail price. So we both came out ahead.

Used furniture may save money. Companies also need furniture for each person's office, for the reception area and for the conference rooms and for the break room. There are many options to consider. Companies are constantly going out of business and have furniture to sell or sometimes give it away just to get it hauled out of a facility that is being closed. Watch the papers for ads. Sometimes other business associates will circulate the news.

When I opened one of my businesses, I reviewed ads in the paper and found furniture that was perfect for my reception area. The people selling it were going through a divorce and were liquidating all of the furniture in the house. I was able to purchase an entire living room set for a fraction of the new retail price. I had to be ready to pay cash and transport the furniture myself.

Purchasing used furniture and equipment on the Internet through sites such as EBay offers another option as well.

Furniture rent to own. There are companies that will rent to own. Remember in leasing furniture, just as in leasing a car, someone else is making money to purchase and finance the items for you. However, if capital is an issue and time is of the essence to have your business up and running, this may be the best option. Again run the numbers and decide where your capital should be spent.

Business equipment must be acquired or leased. Copiers and fax machines are necessary for any business as well. Be careful in deciding which model or brand to purchase or lease. Many times the machine may seem relatively inexpensive, but the toner and consumable items are very expensive. It may be cheaper in the long run to pay a little more for the machine and pay less per item for the toner cartridges. I once purchased a combination copier and computer printer that was on the "sale" table for half price. The cost of the expensive toner cartridges more than used up the savings on the purchases price of the equipment.

Computer systems are required for businesses. Computer systems are required for companies to compete in today's world. This is not an area that you want to try and pay the cheapest price. You want to negotiate certainly, but the parameters and the specs that you need to operate your business should not be short changed. Having a system that runs efficiently and quickly will save you more money in the long run. You and your employees will spend less time at the computer and more time promoting your products and services. Buy the state of the art processors and more memory than you think that you will need. Consult with your Information Technology Consultant, (ITC), to obtain the correct equipment for your business. I have an entire chapter devoted to this selection process. See Chapter 9, *Technology*, for more information.

Consider lease/purchase. Many companies offer the option of leasing these systems as well. Consider a lease purchase instead of straight lease if purchasing is not a possibility. Many times the payout is only a dollar at the end of the lease. Make sure that you plan on keeping the asset for the life of the lease.

Depreciation and direct expense elections for purchases. One of the advantages of purchasing equipment and certain vehicles is that as a small business, you can qualify to direct expense capital expenditures, instead of capitalizing and depreciating the asset over a number of years. This direct expense election, or Section 179 election, is available to small business owners that do not invest more than a certain amount. For 2006, the maximum amount that could be invested during the year without reduction in the expense election was $430,000. The direct expense that was allowed for 2006, was the amount spent up to the income of the company or $108,000, SUV limit is $25,000. There are other limitations depending on your legal entity. *Consult www.MyBreadAndButter.com for annual updates and other tax downloads.*

Maximize the section 179 tax election. A tax planning strategy both in starting a business and each year that you are in business, is to maximize this Section 179 election to reduce income and save taxes. This election is only available for purchased not leased items. Therefore, there is a significant advantage to purchasing an asset, if you write off all or a large part of the purchase price in the first year and save current year tax dollars. Especially if you purchase the asset at the end of the year and have not had to pay for it yet and are able to write it off and save tax dollars and use future earnings to pay for it.

Only purchase what you need. You only want to purchase what you need, not just to spend money to save taxes. I have had clients so proud that they saved tax dollars, but then didn't use what they bought. If it costs a dollar to save $.40 in taxes, you are still out the other $.60 for the item. It would have been cheaper to pay the taxes and have the $.60 left over to buy something that you really needed or to invest for your retirement.

Run the numbers and explore all options before deciding whether to lease or purchase. Lee had a number of options to consider before leasing his car and if he had considered them he may have made different choices.

The bottom line is that by doing your research and exploring all of the options available you will be able to save money and find the right option for you and your business.

BUYING VS LEASING CHECKLIST

	Strategy	Page Ref #	Application To Your Business
1.	Title the car in business if use more than 50% for business use	183	
2.	Purchase the car whenever possible	184	
3.	Leasing causes a liability and no asset on the balance sheet	184	
4.	No residual value when lease is terminated	184	
5.	Must pay balance of lease payments if terminate early	184	
6.	Headaches of ownership without the rights	184	
7.	May have to pay sales tax on the interest	185	
8.	Mileage overages are expensive on leases	185	
9.	Sometimes it is "OK" to lease	185	
10.	When a leased car is totaled, the balance of lease payments are still due to be paid	185	
11.	Negotiate the best cash deal first	185	

	Strategy	Page Ref #	Application To Your Business
12.	Be prepared to walk out of the dealership and to double check numbers	186	
13.	May consider leasing phone systems, furniture and computer systems	186	
14.	Phone systems should have features that will save time and allow your employees to be efficient	186	
15.	Used furniture may save money	187	
16.	Furniture rent to own	187	
17.	Business equipment must be acquired or leased	187	
18.	Computer systems are required for business	187	
19.	Consider lease/purchase	188	
20.	Depreciation and direct expense elections for purchases	188	
21.	Maximize the section 179 tax election	188	
22.	Only purchase what you need	189	
23.	Run the numbers and explore all options before deciding whether to lease or purchase	189	

CHAPTER 17
Customer Service

David owned an electronic store near a mall and had fifteen employees. Trying to be efficient with the fewest number of employees, he chose to use electronics as much as possible. When you called the store, your call was answered by voice mail, with a number of options to pick and then several answer trees before you could leave a message. When customers called in they had to know what they wanted before going into the answer tree otherwise they couldn't find what they wanted.

David didn't schedule anyone to answer the phone for the times a caller did manage to find the operator key to ask someone for help. A message was left which David reviewed a couple of times a day and then he returned the calls himself. The website was very busy and hard to follow. The sales staff on duty on the store floor were told to stay at their stations and just point to locations when customers asked where certain products were located. They could service more customers by having them come to the employee instead of the employee going to the customers. Business had been dropping off and David thought that he could make up sales during the Holiday season, but that didn't happen either. David didn't understand what went wrong.

You only have one opportunity to make a first impression. Whether the first impression is over the phone or in person, if your potential customer or client doesn't have a good impression of your company, it will be hard to change their opinion. The person who is your first point of contact, whether as an operator on the phone or as a receptionist in your office, is the most important person in your company. Unfortunately this person tends to be paid the least and have the least company experience. This person needs to be trained in role-playing and should be given strategies to handle difficult callers.

You should call you office at least once a month and see how your phone is answered and also have friends or colleagues call to see how they are treated and give you their feedback. One idea I have gotten from a past seminar is to give your 'point person' the title "Director of First Impressions." This will hopefully give them a sense of how important they really are and the importance of taking this responsibility seriously.

Voice mail is impersonal. Voice mail is frustrating and impersonal. If you know what you want to ask the store and have the patience to work through the decision trees and recordings, good for you — but many people do not have this virtue. If a potential customer becomes frustrated and they have other choices, they may choose not to do business with you. I recommend having a live person answer the phone when the caller pushes zero. That way, when your customer becomes confused or frustrated and pushes zero, they will be relieved to talk with a live person and will likely continue to do business with your company.

If David had a live person to answer the phone when customers were frustrated with the phone tree, he might have saved some of his customers. If customers are required to leave a message and wait for a return call they will probably go to the competition.

On some automated voicemail systems, pushing zero doesn't work to get to the operator. They make you listen to the entire recording (assuming that you wait that long) to find out that seven or nine is the operator number. If your customer has a limited amount of time to call your company because they are on a break from work or they got off work a few minutes before 5pm to call the company, they may not have enough time to work through all of your recordings. As the owner of the company, think about what you would like to happen to you if you were calling another store. Cutting corners in personnel does not always increase your bottom line, if it causes you to lose sales and revenue. Considered from this perspective, the additional personnel cost may be worth it.

Email is a great but impersonal way to communicate; ensure emails are answered in a timely manner. Email has totally changed the way that we do business. I have some clients who won't talk with anyone on the phone any more; they will only communicate by email. That is great if you are at your computer all day long. If you are on the road visiting customers or clients, however, responding to emails on a timely basis may be more difficult.

I have finally purchased a cell phone that receives my email too. Now, when I am out of the office (and it is working properly), I can at least review email and either call the sender or make a short response before I return to the office. I use emails for setting up appointments instead of calling and spending time on the phone while the person looks up their calendar, etc. One aspect to recognize about emails is that they are one-sided and not a continuous interactive discussion. Clients or customers who have quick questions that can be answered with short answers or don't require questions to be asked of them in return are appropriate emails. If you don't ask your questions and, as a result, make assumptions about your client's situation, you could answer the wrong question. Set up email protocol within your company and outside the company. Set up email addresses that the company controls, so that if the employee leaves, you have access to their email for responding to new emails and staying in touch with your clients.

Websites are a necessity. Websites are valuable tools for your customers to learn more about your business, your qualifications and your products and services. A website can be interactive, allowing customers to ask questions, order products and services, and monitor orders and status. Customers can download forms and other resources. You can post links to other resources for their convenience. If the customer sends you an email or orders a product or service off the website, it is important to have an auto-responder send an email thanking them for their order or email and explaining what will happen next and when. See Chapter 12, *Internet Marketing and Websites*, for more specific information on this topic.

David should "clean up" the busy website and make it easy to navigate.

Stay connected with your customer base with e-newsletters. When you obtain a customer, whether on the Internet or in your store, request their email address. This information is almost more important than their phone number. Develop an e-newsletter that provides education and doesn't necessarily try to sell them anything. They will appreciate that you are educating them, and they will be connected to your company, so that when they need your products or services, they will remember you. Additionally, when you have a new product or service to offer, you'll have a friendly customer to inform and they will be more likely to consider purchasing it from you.

David should consider collecting email addresses and staying in contact with his customers with e-newsletters.

Handle complaints with an ear and a smile. You may have heard the saying that the customer is always right. Well that might not be totally right, but they need to feel that they could be right. They need to have someone listen to them and acknowledge their feelings. They want someone to care that they are upset and to take responsibility for solving their problem and to be nice to them.

If they are on the phone, if you smile while you are talking with them, your demeanor will come across in a pleasant way. It is also harder to fuss or complain when you are smiling. Don't allow them to get off the phone or leave the store without a plan of action on your part to resolve their issues. Then follow through and communicate. If you tell them you are going to call them tomorrow, call them tomorrow, even if you have nothing new to report. Even if you can't resolve their problem, the fact that you tried to resolve it is what they will remember most about the company and may be willing to give the company another chance in the future.

Don't put the "adult diapers" on the top shelf. I had an elderly family member complain one time that she was using a scooter to shop in the grocery store and when she arrived at the aisle that had the adult diapers, they were on the top shelf. She asked me if I knew any really tall elderly people or any who were agile enough to reach up and knock something off the top shelf. She also wondered how many they actually sold and what would happen if they put them on a lower shelf. Think about your customer and what will make it easier for them to purchase your products or services.

Keep the store clean and neat. One of the most distracting things about shopping in a store is noticing dirt and trash on the floor and in the corners. It is an uncomfortable feeling and I don't want to stay in the store very long as I begin to feel dirty too. People are generally more comfortable about spending more time browsing in a clean and neat store. Some customers may not care, but some will, and you don't want to give any customers a reason not to do business with you.

Don't clean around your customers. It drives me crazy to be in a restaurant or a retail store and when it is close to closing time they start running the vacuum cleaner. In restaurants, they interrupt your conversations to get the condiments off your table to refill them and then put them back on the table. Whether I have chosen to purchase goods or services when you first open the doors or when you are about to close them, I should have the opportunity to have the same experience with the products, services, and location. I don't think about the fact that I stayed until closing time; instead I believe that I am not important enough as a customer to be left alone to enjoy my meal or finish my shopping without interruption.

Call customers by name. I enjoy going to stores where there are greeters at the front door. I am in a happy mood as I walk in the store and I am looking forward to a positive experience. When I pay for the products with a credit card and the clerk responds when handing me my card back by calling me by name and thanking me for my business, I feel more connected to the store and maybe a little more important to them as a customer. They are taking the time to call me by name.

The Golden Rule. We've all heard it before: *Do unto others what you would like to have done unto you.* In other words, treat others the way that you would want to be treated. If you don't want to be treated that particular way, don't treat someone else that way. This is a simple rule that goes a long way in business and in life.

Set up appointments instead of long wait lines. No one likes to stand in lines or wait for any kind of service. We live in an instantaneous world, so working to eliminate the wait time is important to retain customers. Restaurants that have reservations or a "call ahead" program reduce the wait time. Some restaurants give you pagers that allow you to shop in neighboring stores while you wait. Recently the new Georgia Aquarium opened and when you purchase your tickets, you sign up for a particular appointment time to enter the facility. Picking up numbers and estimated times to return to the ticket booth has also been used in selling tickets for other popular venues. Be creative and work toward reducing wait times for your customers.

Go the extra mile, it is never crowded. I read this on a rock outside a doctor's office and it struck me as profound. Why not set your company apart from the competition, and go that extra mile? Many companies are so concerned with making money, that they justify reducing staff and service to supposedly improve their bottom line. Why not allow employees to spend the time to go the extra mile and see if the bottom line increases with this method? I know that sometimes this relationship between service and revenue is hard to quantify. If the employee spends a few extra minutes, does that relate to "x" dollars in sales? Consider this; it stands to reason that if you please a customer, they will want to spend money on that trip and then come back and spend money again and again.

If you can't serve the customer, find someone who can. I decided to purchase a success calendar for my employees and "A" clients one year. I visited my office supply store and they did not have enough for the number that I needed. This clerk looked on the computer and found all of the other stores in a reasonable distance and listed how many were at each store. She then called each store to make sure the computer inventory was correct and then asked them to set them aside with my name on it. We still did not have enough, so she called her competition and asked them to set them aside for me as well. I keep going to that store and whenever possible I stop and speak to this clerk and she helps whenever she is there and I have questions. I am very loyal to that store because of her.

Customers like to know what to expect. Fast food franchises are known for their standardized food menu. When I visited Japan and went into a popular hamburger franchise, I knew that I was going to get a hamburger fixed the same way as if I ordered it at home in Kennesaw, Georgia. There is some comfort in knowing this, as opposed to taking a chance on another restaurant and not getting something that I want. This is true for floor layouts in grocery stores etc. I know that the grocery store that I normally visit has a basic floor plan that is standard in all of the stores in the area. So if I need to run in another store I have an idea which direction I need to go from the front door and I don't spend precious minutes going up and down all of the isles. So I will visit this chain more often than another chain when I am out of my home area.

The shopping experience needs to be pleasant. If you have a pleasant experience you tend to spend more money. My most favorite shopping trip was in New York City. I was in town on business to make presentations to Moody's and Standard and Poors and I had a couple of hours between my last meeting and my dinner appointment. I asked the cab driver to pick a place to take me and to consider that I didn't like to shop, but I wanted to experience New York City in a positive way.

He took me to a boutique mall. I found a petite store and I walked in and they immediately greeted me. A sales person started walking around with me and wanted to know all about what I was looking for and what I wanted. After asking a series of questions about my favorite colors and styles she delivered me to a dressing room and asked what kind of wine I would like. I spent the next hour and half with wine and cheese and crackers and being waited on by the most concerned sales person I have ever met. I did not leave the dressing room until I was finished, she brought me suits and dresses and accessories. I expressed my likes and dislikes and she adjusted her selections accordingly.

I didn't really plan on spending money on this shopping adventure, it was just an opportunity to kill a couple of hours and not stay in the hotel room. I found a number of suits and dresses with accessories that were just perfect for me and I was enjoying myself so much that I WANTED to buy the clothes. I spent over $1,000 in 1989 on this shopping spree. I haven't spent that much at one time since and I also have never had that kind of experience in another store since. I was happy and I believed that the salesperson really cared about me and that she wanted to make me happy through her concern and care in the choices of clothes that she brought me.

If that store was in Atlanta, I would buy all of my clothes there. It was a total shopping experience. Was it worth it for that sales person to spend that hour and half with me for $1,000? I believe that the manager of any store would be willing to make that exchange of an employee's time and attention for a client's business every single day.

Personnel available to answer questions for customers. There are several home improvement stores in my area. As a female I go into these stories knowing that I need something to fix what I have that is broken, but I don't always know what it is that I exactly need to buy. I have found that in one of the stores, it is difficult to find someone who will talk with me, and if they do, they treat me like I am stupid and I find that I don't want to go in that store at all. The other store tends to have more employees on the floor and they come to me to ask if they can help me. I feel uncomfortable trying to figure things out, but I am not stupid, so having a friendly employee who treats me as someone who is capable of understanding what I need as they explain it to me is very empowering. I am more willing to stay in the store, suffer through figuring things out and actually buy what it is that I need to fix what's broken.

If David doesn't provide enough personnel to answer questions for his customers and check them out in a timely basis, they will not buy from him.

Take the customer to the product that they need and take responsibility for the customer until they are satisfied. I was in an electronics store recently and asked what kind of memory cards the store had in stock that would work with my cell phone. The clerk raised his hand and pointed over to the right and said that they were two isles over. I asked him to show me, he heaved a heavy sigh and stomped over to the isle and then started to walk away after pointing to a wall of memory cards. I had to call him back and ask him to help me figure out which one I actually needed for my particular phone. He looked at me and said that he would have to get someone else.

I waited a few minutes in front of the isle and someone else showed up and then pointed to a couple of memory cards and told me that they might work. I asked who would know which one would work and he said that I needed to go to the camera department. I had to ask him to take me there and introduce me to someone who could help me. The camera clerk was helpful and I finally selected a memory card based on his recommendation. If I had not been told by the cellular company that the card I needed was at this particular electronic franchise, I would have gone somewhere else after the first encounter with the first careless clerk. I felt like I had to fight to learn enough to finally spend my money. I won't go into this store again without someone who understands what I need with me. I would rather go somewhere else.

Suggestion box. Consider having a suggestion box for employees to make suggestions anonymously. Many times they have terrific suggestions, as they are on the floor or in direct contact with the customers every day and will have ideas about how your company could better serve your customers. You may want to have a contest for ideas that generate income or reduce expenses or better serve customers, and reward an employee each month or reward each employee for their ideas based on the value to the company. My father made extra money each month, which was paid to him in proportion to the money he saved for his company. Allow your employees to be the eyes and ears of you and the company, and empower them to make a difference. You may be surprised what you discover to improve your business.

Be sensitive to learning and physical disabilities. It is so important to be sensitive to the learning and physical disabilities of your customers. I took my car in to be serviced a few years ago and the service manager had a handlebar mustache and fired off questions at an elderly lady while looking down at her service order. The elderly lady kept saying "huh, huh," so he started yelling back at her. Finally, he looked up and yelled the questions to her. She jumped and eventually she answered his questions. She left looking very upset and bewildered. When it was my turn, I mentioned to the service manager that I didn't think that she could hear him and that I thought that she had to read his lips to answer his questions. He paused and realized that I might have been right and he hadn't thought about the reason they were having problems communicating.

Sometimes customers don't mean to be difficult to work with, they just can't help it. I also have a family member who has learning disabilities in reading and spelling. He has a difficult time reading and figuring out words but he has a gifted IQ. So, he is not going to read signs or instructions no matter how many are put up or given to him. Having another way to obtain the information, such as a tape recording or someone who is willing to walk him through the steps or process would keep him as a customer for the long term. Learning disabilities are not uncommon and these customers have money to spend as well.

"That is easy." In an effort to comfort someone learning a new skill or an area that is out of their expertise, sometimes the words "oh, that is easy," is used. I purchased a new general ledger software program for my CPA practice to use with my clients' books. Every time I asked a question about how to do something in the software, the trainer would say, "oh, that is easy". I would immediately feel stupid and angry, like I was not capable of figuring out something that she proclaimed was easy. I kept suggesting that she use different words.

In this circumstance, I suggest saying to your customer, "I can help you with that." Then they will not feel stupid, but rather capable of understanding what will be explained to them. Another set of words that gives a positive feeling is to respond to a customer's thanks with, "it is my pleasure", instead of "you are welcome". "You are welcome" is courteous and nice, but "it is my pleasure" is wonderful. Words solicit responses from your emotions and if you train your employees to use the words that generate positive emotions instead of negative emotions, it will affect your business in a positive way.

Unhappy customers tell other potential customers. To this day I have never purchased another piece of software from the software company described in the previous passage that sent that unpleasant trainer to my office. I have told other CPA's the story and still share it when someone states that they are thinking about buying software from that company. Unhappy customers never forget and they make sure others don't forget either.

Train, retrain, and remind your employees. All of these concepts are great, but just telling employees to do these things is not enough. You have to have them practice, and practice some more to develop habits that are natural and genuine.

Invest time and money in providing customer service. Yes, this takes time and money. But it doesn't make sense to spend the marketing dollars to have potential customers or clients call you or come to your store, only to lose them due to poor customer service. Employees only care about what you care about, make customer service a priority, and monitor and reward their performance. So choose to care about customer service, and your employees will too.

David should implement these customer service ideas and he will see an improvement in his business.

CUSTOMER SERVICE CHECKLIST

	Strategy	Page Ref #	Application To Your Business
1.	You only have one opportunity to make a first impression	194	
2.	Voice mail is impersonal	194	
3.	Email is a great but impersonal way to communicate; ensure emails are answered in a timely manner	195	
4.	Websites are a necessity	195	
5.	Stay connected with your customer base with e-newsletters	196	
6.	Handle complaints with an ear and a smile	196	
7.	Don't put the "adult diapers" on the top shelf	196	
8.	Keep the store clean and neat	197	
9.	Don't clean around your customers	197	
10.	Call customers by name	197	
11.	The Golden Rule	197	
12.	Set up appointments instead of long wait lines	198	

	Strategy	Page Ref #	Application To Your Business
13.	Go the extra mile, it is never crowded	198	
14.	If you can't serve the customer, find someone that can	198	
15.	Customers like to know what to expect	199	
16.	The shopping experience needs to be pleasant	199	
17.	Personnel available to answer questions for customers	200	
18.	Take the customer to the product that they need and take responsibility for the customer until they are satisfied	200	
19.	Suggestion box	201	
20.	Be sensitive to learning and physical disabilities	201	
21.	"That is easy"	202	
22.	Unhappy customers tell other potential customers	202	
23.	Train, retrain, and remind your employees	202	
24.	Invest time and money in providing customer service	203	

CHAPTER 18
Retirement Plans

Liz started her law firm five years ago and she has done very well. She has a Sub-Chapter S Corporation. Her salary for the year was $150,000 and she has $100,000 in net income for the year. She also has paid two employees who have been with her over five years a total of $80,000 in salary for the year deducted before the net income of $100,000. She would like to reduce her taxable income and plan for her retirement.

This Chapter includes tax information for the tax year of 2006, in some cases these limits will still apply for 2006 returns filed during the extension period. Some 2007 limitations are included and full updated information for 2007 and future years can be downloaded from www.RunASuccessfulBusiness.com.

Seek tax advice before adopting a retirement plan. The tax advice in this chapter is very general and you should consult with your CPA to obtain specific recommendations for your company and situation.

Qualified retirement plans. Qualified retirement plans allow employers and employees to contribute to these plans and receive a deferred or preferred tax treatment for the contributions and earnings accumulated over time in these accounts. To receive this special tax treatment for the plans, participants have to qualify through the employer and the employer must follow specific rules outlined by Congress and enforced by the IRS.

Favorable tax treatment for qualified retirement plans. As a general rule the contributions to employer qualified retirement plans are tax deductible by the employer and not income to the employee until they withdraw the money from the plan. The earnings are not taxed during the year that they are earned, but are tax deferred until they are withdrawn from the plan. This allows for the earnings to accumulate as pre-tax dollars and the plan can earn income on the money that would normally be withdrawn out of taxable investment to pay the taxes each year. So both the plan earnings and the tax money can earn income without requiring withdrawals for income taxes during eligible years. Employees are generally eligible to receive employer contributions from 21 years of age until 70 1/2 years of age based on meeting either hours of service, year of service or annual income amounts, depending on the qualified plan.

Non-discrimination rules apply to these plans. Generally employers want to contribute to qualified retirement plans for themselves and their families but may not realize that they must cover all of their eligible employees in the same way as well. So if the desired contribution rate is 25% of qualified salary of the owner, then 25% must be contributed for the eligible employees' salaries as well. All eligible employees must be treated the same. Therefore, some employers forego contributions believing that the amount for the eligible employees is too large compared to the amount to be contributed for the owner/employee. I encourage employers to remember the amount that is required by the plan to be contributed for the employees is tax deductible. Subtract the tax savings from the employer contribution for the employees and determine the net after tax cost of this amount to the business. Then compute the owner/employee contribution and the related tax savings. If the net after tax cost of the employee contribution is less than the tax savings for the employer's portion's tax savings, the employer is coming out ahead even after contributing for the employees. Assuming the cash is available the employer should do it. If it still cost more for the employees, the employer may want to consider paying the maximum contributions to keep employees happy and working for the company.

Choose an individual as your beneficiary for your retirement account. Choose an individual as your beneficiary for your retirement account instead of your estate. Since the estate tax tables climb very quickly to the maximum tax bracket, your estate will usually pay more in income taxes than someone in your family. By choosing an individual or individuals as the beneficiary of your plan account, the balance will generally be withdrawn over a much longer period of time. Whether a lump sum or payments over several years, your individual beneficiaries will generally pay less income tax than the estate. See your CPA for more specific tax planning.

Most employer retirement plans are tax deferred not tax exempt. Most employer retirement plans are tax deferred not tax exempt and the employee is expected to pay the taxes on the balance in the plan as it is withdrawn during their lifetime. Therefore, someone or some entity will pay income taxes on the balances in these plans.

Required to start withdrawing at 70 1/2 based on required minimum distribution tables. The general rule is that participants are required to start withdrawing from their qualified retirement accounts by April 1 of the year after the year in which they turn 70 1/2. They are to refer to the required minimum distribution tables each year to determine the factor that must be used to calculate the required minimum distribution for that year. This forces the employee to pay taxes during their lifetime as discussed above.

May want to withdraw before 70 1/2 to pay lower income taxes. Participants may not want to wait to withdraw the retirement funds in the plan. If the beneficiaries are in higher tax brackets than the retired participant, they may want to start withdrawing in their 60's and spread the withdrawals over a number of tax years to keep the taxes as low as possible. This is ripe for tax planning to minimize the taxes due and the most left over for the beneficiaries after paying taxes.

Employer qualified plans and IRAs are subject to estate taxes at death as well. When someone dies all of the assets and liabilities are counted and they may be subject to estate taxes on their assets less their liabilities. If the decedent has a taxable estate the balance in the retirement plans may be subject to estate taxes as well as the income taxes normally paid on withdrawals. This is an area that requires extensive planning and I recommend that you contact your CPA to assist you in minimizing your estate and income taxes as it relates to these plans.

Employee vesting in qualified plans. Employer contributions may be immediately vested or may have graduated vesting schedules over a five-year period. Employee contributions are generally immediately vested. Vesting means that the employee has earned all of the rights to take the balance in their participant account with them when they leave the company.

Employee withdrawals may be taxed. If an employee withdraws their money from the qualified plan and does not roll it over into another plan, it is taxable to them in the year of the withdrawal. Generally if the employee is less than 59 1/2 years of age at the time of the withdrawal then a penalty of 10% will be due for early withdrawal. This money was given favorable tax treatment as it was to be used for your retirement. Generally if you withdraw it before normal retirement age you have not used it for your retirement and therefore are subject to penalties to make up for the favorable tax treatment.

Rollovers can delay taxation of qualified plan investments. If you leave an employer and want to have control of your retirement investments, you can transfer the balance in your account directly to an Individual Retirement Account. As long it is rolled over from institution to institution and doesn't go through your hands or if you do receive a check made payable to you, and roll it into an IRA within 60 days of the date of the check, there are no taxes or penalties due for this transaction at this time.

Exceptions to early withdrawal penalties. There are a few exceptions to the early withdrawal penalty. These include:

1) Distributions through a Qualified Domestic Relations Order (QDRO), as a result of a divorce
2) Converting the account into an annuity payment stream based on specific rules
3) Death
4) Disability

Consult your CPA to see if you will qualify for any exceptions before you withdraw the money.

Loans to employees. Retirement accounts are not designed to be savings accounts to be used prior to retirement. Some companies recognize the employees plan to plan for retirement, but sometimes life throws the best planner curve balls. So they provide for short term loans generally one to five years for unusual events that would qualify for a loan. These events may be unusual medical costs, catastrophic events to home or loved one, or other unusual events that would be eligible for a loan from the plan. These allow the participant to repay themselves and to get back on their feet without incurring a tax liability by just withdrawing the money from the plan.

Leaving employer will cause loans to be taxable. If you leave your employer and still have an outstanding loan in your qualified plan, it will be treated as a distribution to you and become immediately taxable and may be subject to penalties as explained above. Pay off loans before resigning from the company. Borrow the money somewhere else if you have to avoid the taxes and penalties.

Take responsibility for your own retirement. If employers offer you opportunities to participate in qualified retirement plans adjust your budget so that you can participate to the maximum amounts allowed by the plan. If your employer does not have a plan or you do not qualify to participate yet, contribute to your own Individual Retirement Plans, IRAs. It is your future and you should take responsibility for it.

Large and small companies can have qualified retirement plans. With the variety of qualified retirement plans available to employers, the small companies can have plans just like the large companies. This will allow smaller companies to compete with the larger companies for employees that are looking for these benefits from their employer.

Start early and let compounding work its magic. Lee, a 20 year old, invests $4,000 per year into his Individual Retirement Account (IRA) for 10 years and then stops making contributions. With a fixed 5% rate of return compounded daily he will have $306,195 at age 65. Tina, a 30 year old invests $4,000 per year into her IRA for 20 years and then stopped making contributions. With a fixed 5% rate of return compounded daily Tina will have $296,773 at age 65. Why does Lee who contributed for only 10 years have more money than Tina, who contributed for 20 years? The magic of compounding interest grew Lee's investment for a longer period of time. The sooner you start saving and investing in your future the more that you can potentially have to provide income during your retirement years. Since these accounts are qualified retirement plans, and there have been no withdrawals, no taxes are due during this accumulation period under current law.

Younger adults believe that they will live forever. Younger adults believe that that they will live forever and retirement is a long way off. It is hard for them to imagine not being able to go find a job and make money when they need it. They want to buy cars, houses and boats and have fun. If they sacrifice a little fun when they are young, they won't have to sacrifice as much as when they are closer to retirement. When they reach their 40's and 50's, and realize that they haven't saved anything and now need to save as much as they can for as long as they can. Show examples to your children and to your young adult employees and encourage them to let time and tax deferral do the work for them.

Individuals are living longer in retirement. The retirement plan used to be that you worked all of your life, retired at 65, went on a cruise and then you died. Now individuals are living 20 to 30 years in retirement and with modern medicine they may live even longer in the years to come. My great uncles retired at age 62 from a grocery store that they owned. They lived to be 91 and 92. They lived 50% again in retirement as they had lived and worked prior to retirement. They worked approximately 40 years to provide for 30 years in retirement. Now, we might be working 45 years to provide for 45 years in retirement. This requires planning, discipline and sacrifice for today to provide for tomorrow.

Budget for retirement plan contributions. Retirement plan contributions should be considered as part of employee and owner compensation and should be budgeted with the regular salary amounts. A client admitted to me once that he wished that when he purchased his first business after leaving the big corporate world, that someone had told him that not budgeting for his retirement plan contribution was not an option. His previous employer had paid into a pension plan for him each year and he had not had to consider retirement plan contributions for himself and didn't plan for them working for this employer. Now he was on his own and didn't know that he should be setting up a plan for the company and contributing to it. Please consult your tax and financial advisors for you options and how much to budget for your contributions for you and your employees.

Find money to save. If all we had to do was "get rid" of our cash, we would all be in good shape. Most of us do a great job of spending it, just not saving it. How can the average person "find" money to save? If you are 30 years old and if you could eliminate purchases that throw away money such as purchasing lottery tickets or purchasing expensive coffees or buying candy. Just $3 per day or $90 per month invested at a fixed rate of return of 5% for 35 years compounded daily would accumulate $102,486. This is $100,000 that you would not have, if you had not "found" the money to do it. Just think about what the number would be if you could afford to invest more each month.

Types of qualified employer retirement plans. The types of plans that may be considered by small business employers are:

1) Simplified Employee Pension (SEP)Plan,
2) Savings Incentive Match for Employees (SIMPLE) Plan,
3) Profit Sharing Plan,
4) Comparability Profit Sharing Plan,
5) Defined Benefit Plan,
6) 401-(k) Plan,
7) Safe Harbor 401 (k) Plan,
8) Individual (k) Plan.

Simplified Employee Pension (SEP) Plan. Simplified Employee Pension (SEP) Plans are best suited for an Owner who has few or no employees and wants a plan this relatively simple and inexpensive to install and administer. The employer pays entire contribution for the employee, and new plans do not allow for employee contributions. The owner can elect to contribute for all eligible employees from zero to 25% of eligible salaries each year. There is no requirement for a contribution each year. The maximum eligible contribution for this plan for 2006 is $44,000 per employee and for 2007 is $45,000 per employee. This plan can be established after the end of the year. See www.RunASuccessfulBusiness.com for annual updates and other tax information downloads.

Savings Incentive Match for Employees (SIMPLE) Plan. SIMPLE plans can't have more than 100 employees and this plan is also relatively simple and inexpensive to install and administer. This plan allows for employees to contribute up to $10,000 (2006) or $10,500 (2007) of their salary if they are under 50 and the employee can contribute an additional $2,500 (2006 and 2007) if they are over 50. Under this plan the employer has a matching requirement and can make certain elections under the plan. Generally the employer's contribution compared to other plans is a very small percentage of the employee's contribution. This allows owners who want to contribute up to $10,000 (2006) or $10,500 (2007) and if over 50 the extra $2,500 for themselves, and who don't have the resources to contribute comparable amounts for the other employees to do so. Some employees may want to contribute and some may not. This allows a vehicle for those employees who do want to plan and contribute for their retirement as well, even if the employer does not plan to contribute more than the minimum required amount. Employer contributions are not elective and are set at the beginning of the tax year and the employer is committed based on what the employees decided to contribute.

Profit Sharing Plan. As with SEP Plans, contributions to a Profit sharing plan are flexible in that there are no requirements for a contribution each year. The contribution is zero to 25% of eligible salaries for all eligible employees. Generally there are one or a few higher paid employee/owners and other non-owner employees. The maximum eligible contribution for this plan for 2006 is $44,000 and for 2007 is $45,000 per employee.

Comparability Profit Sharing Plan. Generally if the owners are older than the other employees and there are several groups or classes of employees, then the comparability profit sharing plan is the option selected.

Contributions are still flexible and not required and may be between zero to 25 percent of eligible compensation each year. The difference in this plan is that the contribution pool may not be distributed as a flat percentage of all eligible salaries. The classes and formulas may allow more of the pool as a percentage to go to the older owners as a class than the younger class of employees. The maximum eligible contribution for this plan for 2006 is $44,000 and for 2007 is $45,000 per employee.

Defined Benefit Plan. A defined benefit plan has mandatory contributions each year based on a formula that an actuary has determined per eligible employee. This plan is generally adopted by owners who are in their 50's or above and the rest of the employees are significantly younger. The owners need to save as much as possible for their retirement and their business is expected to make enough each year to fund the required contributions each year. The maximum salary that can be considered in the actuary computations is $175,000 for 2006 and $180,000 for 2007.

401-(k) Plan. Generally considered by companies that have 25 or more employees and want to allow the employee's to elect to defer part of their salary. The higher paid owners want to participate, but will be limited by the contribution elections made by the general employee pool. The employer may match or add a profit sharing contribution to each employee's participant account. The maximum eligible contribution for the total of the employee and employer for this plan for 2006 is $44,000 and for 2007 is $45,000 per employee. The maximum employee contribution for 2006 is $15,000 and for 2007 is $15,500 and $20,000 for 2006 and $20,500 for 2007 for employees over 50.

Safe Harbor 401 (k) Plan. Generally considered by companies that have 25 or more employees and want to provide an employee deferral piece and the higher paid owners want to participate, but may have limitations in a regular 401 (k) plan. This contribution is mandatory each year, but it is not subject to the top heavy limitations for highly paid employees that the regular 401 (k) plans are subject to. The maximum eligible contribution for the total of the employee and employer for this plan for 2006 is $44,000 and for 2007 is $45,000 per employee. The maximum employee contribution for 2006 is $15,000 and for 2007 is $15,500 and $20,000 for employees over 50 for both years.

Individual (k) Plan. Owners who have no employees other than a spouse may consider this plan. This plan has an employee tax deferral piece up to $15,000 for 2006 and $15,500 for 2007 if under 50 and an employer contribution as well. The maximum, combined employer and employee, eligible contributions for this plan for 2006 is $44,000 and for 2007 is $45,000 per employee. The advantage to this plan over the SIMPLE or SEP plans is that most Individual (k) plans allow for loans to the employee of their vested balance up to $50,000. This provides for a benefit that is normally not available except in large company 401 (k) plans.

What should Liz do? Since it's already after the end of the year and Liz wants to cover her 3 employees, Liz should consider a SEP plan. She should consider contributing 25% of both her salary and the employees' salaries into the plan. Her contribution would be 25% of $150,000 (only salary counts, not net income form a Sub-S Corporation) or $37,500, her tax savings would be $14,425 as she is in the 39% state and federal tax bracket. The employees' contribution would be 25% of $80,000 would be $20,000, but the tax savings is $7,800 and the net cost is $12,200 to Liz. This is less than her tax savings for her contribution of $14,425, so she comes out ahead and provides a great benefit for her employees.

Retirement plans benefit employees and employers and should be considered whenever possible by employers. There are a number of choices and variables to consider in selecting a plan. I recommend that you work with a CPA and an investment advisor to accomplish all of the goals of the company, employees, employer and considering the demographics of your specific employee pool and the company resources. Both employees and employers benefit from qualified retirement plans and with the variety of options to consider, employers should consider them whenever possible. Both need to take responsibility for their retirement and let the government assist by providing for the tax deferrals.

This Chapter includes tax information for the tax year of 2006 and 2007, in some cases these limits will still apply

for returns filed during the 2006 extension period. Updated information for 2007 and future years can be downloaded from www.RunASuccessfulBusiness.com. See Appendix D — Retirement Plans for summary of limitations by plan.

RETIREMENT PLANS CHECKLIST

	Strategy	Page Ref #	Application To Your Business
1.	Seek tax advice before adopting a retirement plan	207	
2.	Qualified retirement plans	207	
3.	Favorable tax treatment for qualified retirement plans	208	
4.	Non-discrimination rules apply to these plans	208	
5.	Choose an individual as your beneficiary for your retirement account	209	
6.	Most employer retirement plans are tax deferred not tax exempt	209	
7.	Required to start withdrawing at 70 1/2 based on required minimum distribution tables	209	
8.	May want to withdraw before 70 1/2 to pay lower income taxes	209	
9.	Employer qualified plans and IRAs are subject to estate taxes at death as well	209	
10.	Employee vesting in qualified plans	210	

	Strategy	Page Ref #	Application To Your Business
11.	Employee withdrawals may be taxed	210	
12.	Rollovers can delay taxation of qualified plan investments	210	
13.	Exceptions to early withdrawal penalties	210	
14.	Loans to employees	211	
15.	Leaving employer will cause loans to be taxable	211	
16.	Take responsibility for your own retirement	211	
17.	Large of small companies can have qualified retirement plans	211	
18.	Start early and let compounding work its magic	211	
19.	Younger adults believe that they will live forever	212	
20.	Individuals are living longer in retirement	212	
21.	Budget for retirement plan contributions	212	
22.	Find money to save	213	

	Strategy	Page Ref #	Application To Your Business
23.	Types of qualified employer retirement plans	213	
24.	Simplified Employee Pension (SEP) Plan	213	
25.	Savings Incentive Match for Employees (SIMPLE) Plan	214	
26.	Profit Sharing Plan	214	
27.	Comparability Profit Sharing Plan	214	
28.	Defined Benefit Plan	215	
29.	401-(k) Plan	215	
30.	Safe Harbor 401 (k) Plan	215	
31.	Individual (k) Plan	216	
32.	Retirement plans benefit employees and employers and should be considered whenever possible by employers	216	

This Chapter includes tax information for the tax years of 2006 and 2007, in some cases these limits will still apply for returns filed during the 2006 extension period. Updated information for future years can be downloaded from www.RunASuccessfulBusiness.com.

See Appendix D — Retirement Plans for a summary of limits by plan.

CHAPTER 19
Dealing with the IRS & Other Government Entities

Brickstone, Inc. had a manufacturing plant located in Georgia and sales and administrative offices located in two other states. Jeff, the President, thought that Henry, the Treasurer, was preparing the payroll tax returns, paying the tax liabilities and filing the sales tax returns in all of the states. Henry was located in another state office from Jeff. Jeff contacted a local CPA to assist him with understanding how to read the company financial statements.

The CPA noticed that the payroll and sales tax liabilities appeared to be higher than a liability for one month. After researching the general ledger and tracing liabilities and payments, the CPA informed Jeff that the payroll taxes and sales tax returns had not been paid for over a year. After questioning Henry about the unpaid taxes, he revealed that notices had been received but he didn't know what to do after he had gotten behind in the filing and the payments.

Jeff was horrified that this had happened. If he and the other owners were aware that more cash was needed to run the business, they would have dealt with borrowing more money, the problem was that they did not know.

You may have personal liability. The IRS and the State Departments of Revenue can hold the officers of Brickstone, Inc. personally liable for the trust funds deducted from the employee checks. This is very serious as the company acts as a trustee for the government in collecting the taxes from the employee paychecks and must remit them by the due date. The penalties can be as high as 100% plus interest until paid.

File the delinquent returns as soon as possible. What can Jeff do now? Jeff needs to have the local CPA prepare all of the delinquent payroll and sales tax returns as soon a possible. After preparing the returns, the total taxes, estimated penalties and interest should be calculated. Jeff needs to meet with the other owners to determine the financing to pay these taxes as soon as possible.

Give power of attorneys to the CPA. Power of attorneys for each government entity should be given to the CPA to handle these matters with the IRS and the States. The power of attorney allows the CPA to discuss the confidential information of the business with the IRS directly without having a representative of the business present. The CPA should have a local contact for the IRS and the various States and he or she should contact them and send them the power of attorneys. He or she should make arrangements to file the returns and verify that all prior returns have been filed. They should also verify that the amount assessed for penalties and interest is correct and make sure that any payments that the company has already paid have been properly applied.

Penalties and interest will continue to accrue until the taxes are paid. If the returns are completed and the money for the taxes due is not available yet, the returns should be filed. It will take at least a couple of weeks to process the returns and calculate the penalties and interest due. The penalties and interest will still accrue until the taxes are paid.

Payment plans are possible. If for some reason the money is not available or they are unable to pay the entire balance due, payment plans can be negotiated. All of the delinquent returns must be filed and the taxpayer must be in full compliance with the filing of tax returns before arrangements for less than full payment can be discussed. All of the taxes must be recorded and assessed before the government will discuss an installment plan. The taxpayer must stay in compliance, paying all taxes when due and filing all tax returns by the due dates during the installment plan period, or the installment plan is revoked.

Liens may be filed. The government may file a lien if the taxes can not be paid off in a reasonable period of time. Some agents will work with you to hold off filing a lien and as long as payments are made according to the agreement, they won't file the lien. Interest and penalties continue to accrue until all of the taxes are paid.

Defaulting on an installment payment plan can be cured. If you miss a payment and default on an installment plan, call the IRS. They will generally work with you to reinstate the payment plan. If you ignore the notices, they will exercise their full powers to collect the debt.

Be careful of levies. One of the options that the IRS has to collect the tax debt is to issue a levy against a bank account of the company. When you set up the installment plan one of the questions that must be completed on the application form is your company bank account number and your bank name and address. So if you default they can issue a levy to collect any monies up to the tax liability from this bank account. When the IRS issues levies to the bank, the bank cannot tell you about it until after they have frozen the amount that is requested or the entire balance in the account whichever is less. You are then notified by the bank and you have a certain period of time to prove to the IRS that you have already paid it or to pay it separately to release the funds. This is embarrassing with your bank and can cause checks to be bounced and other businesses that you do business with may know that you are having cash flow problems. Therefore, it is important to communicate with the IRS before levies are issued.

Offer in Compromise is available for certain situations. For other than trustee payroll taxes withheld, such as employer portion of payroll taxes, income taxes or other business and personal taxes assessed, an offer in compromise may be considered. In certain situations when you have minimal business and personal assets or lack a major asset that could be sold to pay the tax liabilities the IRS may consider an application for an offer in compromise. The IRS has to believe that the amount that you are offering is the most that they will receive instead of waiting for installment payments. In certain situations the offer in compromise is appropriate. It won't work in every situation.

Hire an outside CPA. Even if you have a partner or officer who is a CPA or who has an accounting degree and appears to be qualified to handle the government tax filings, it is important to have an outside CPA to consult with the business. This person can oversee the tax filings and make sure that the proper returns are timely filed. This gives comfort to the other partners or owners. If you own the business yourself, many times you are dependent on an employee to file all of these returns and the outside CPA is even more important to oversee these filings.

Consider an outside payroll service. One of the accounting functions that can be easily outsourced from the company office is payroll. There are payroll services and CPA offices that offer these services at a competitive price and free up the accounting staff to do work on activities that assist the owner in making more money. The payroll services include calculating and printing payroll checks, signature stamping payroll checks, preparing payroll tax returns, determining payroll tax deposits and preparing payment checks and year end returns, Forms W-2 and Forms 1099s. Some services will deduct the taxes from your bank account with each payroll and make the payroll tax deposits for the company when they are due. The owner doesn't have to remember the date that they have to go to the bank to make the deposit or mail the monthly and quarterly returns. Some owners don't want someone to have access to their bank account and prefer to manage their cash flow and tax liabilities themselves. Make sure that a system is in place to remember the due dates. The penalties are substantial for being even one day late.

Mark due dates on a calendar. Make sure that you have tax due dates on a master calendar. Assign the monitoring of the tax due dates to a trusted employee. If you utilize ACT or Outlook or another calendar program, set up alarms the day before the due dates and in the morning of the due dates. Although your outside CPA firm should keep you informed of due dates, it is still the owner's responsibility to file returns and pay taxes when due. Ignorance is no excuse when it comes to dealing with the IRS and other government entities.

Set up tickler files. Set up separate tickler files for each government liability and form that must be filed for your business. Examples include:

1) IRS-Form 941, Federal Employee and Employer Tax Return,
2) IRS-Form 940, Federal Employer Unemployment Tax Return,
3) State-Form ____, Employee State Tax Withholding Return,
4) State-Form ____, State Employer Unemployment Tax Return,
5) State-Form ____, State Sales Tax Return,
6) County or City-Form ____, Business License

According to the type of business and industry with which your company operates you may have other specialty tax returns due as well. Check with your CPA to determine all of the tax returns that you are liable to file and their respective due dates.

Read IRS notices. When you receive an IRS notice, it is important to read it as soon as possible and either respond personally or have your CPA respond as soon as possible. Don't assume that the notice is correct. Review your files and determine if the notice is correct. The IRS and other government entities rely on employees to keypunch returns received into the computer and mistakes are sometimes made during this process.

If you believe that your records are correct, copy all of the documentation and prepare a letter outlining your records and the corrections that need to be made to their records. I have found that it is better to use bullet points and not paragraphs in the letter. It is easier for the agent to follow and they can check off the bullet points as they go down the list. Make sure that you circle or mark the appropriate spots on the documentation that corresponds to your bullet points. Attach all of the documentation and keep a complete copy for your files. Send the letter return receipt requested and keep a file of the correspondence and return receipts. If they state that you didn't respond timely, you have the proof.

Don't panic if you are chosen for an IRS audit. It is important not to panic if you are chosen for an IRS audit. Many audits are randomly selected and are routine and are just a matter of providing the information requested. There are different types of IRS audits, a mail audit, an office audit and an audit where the agent comes to your business location.

IRS Mail audits. Mail audits are more common in recent years. A notice is sent to the taxpayer with a list of items that are being audited on the tax return. The taxpayer is required to provide proof for these items and send them to the address on the notice by the date indicated. After reviewing the documentation the IRS may require additional items or send a proposed adjustment letter or send a closing letter. If you receive a proposed adjustment letter and you don't agree with it, you have rights and there is a process to appeal the adjustment. Contact your CPA or tax attorney for your next steps.

An IRS office audit. In an office audit, the IRS sends a letter with an appointment date and a list of items being audited. The taxpayer is expected to show up at the IRS office with the proof of the items being audited.

An IRS business location audit. A business location audit is set up by an IRS agent to visit the business office and perform the audit on campus. The agent can perform the audit at your CPA's office and just have a tour of your business. I don't recommend having an auditor at your office location reviewing your records. It makes employees nervous and disrupts your business.

Don't represent yourself in an audit. It is important to be represented in an audit either by a CPA or a tax attorney. I do not recommend trying to handle an audit yourself. Hire an independent person who is not emotionally involved in the business to answer questions with the agent. You could attempt to answer a question and use words that may cause the IRS agent to believe that something else in the business needs to be investigated. In all three audits listed above, the CPA or tax attorney will communicate with the IRS agent with your power of attorney and provide the information requested and answer their questions.

If they can't answer the questions or need to obtain more information from you the IRS will allow them time to obtain what they need from you. Many times the appointment times that are assigned by the IRS notices are able to be changed to accommodate the CPA or tax attorney's schedule and your ability to get the records together. Your representative will negotiate the new appointment time with the IRS agent.

Keep good records. It is so important to keep good records in your business. Then if you are audited or have to prove that your returns were prepared properly, you have the records to support your position. This reduces stress and anxiety when a notice or audit arrives.

Don't just sign returns that are prepared for you. Don't just sign returns that are prepared for you. Ask questions of the preparer:

1) What issues should I be concerned about?
2) Were there any decisions, assumptions or positions that were made in preparing this return that may be controversial or that I need to be aware of?
3) Are there any records that I need to improve for next year?

Remember, you are responsible for the items reported on the return as the owner or an officer of the business and you need to take that responsibility seriously.

Dealing with the IRS or other Government entity is not something to be afraid of, but a necessary business activity and should be treated with respect and with responsibility. By setting up due dates and tickler files and hiring an outside CPA to oversee all tax filings, you can concentrate on what you do best in your business and work toward making more money.

DEALING WITH THE IRS & OTHER GOVERNMENT ENTITIES CHECKLIST

	Strategy	Page Ref #	Application To Your Business
1.	You may have personal liability	224	
2.	File the delinquent returns as soon as possible	224	
3.	Give power of attorneys to the CPA	224	
4.	Penalties and interest will continue to accrue until the taxes are paid	224	
5.	Payment plans are possible	224	
6.	Liens may be filed	225	
7.	Defaulting on an installment payment plan can be cured	225	
8.	Be careful of levies	225	
9.	Offer in Compromise is available for certain situations	225	
10.	Hire an outside CPA	226	
11.	Consider an outside payroll service	226	
12.	Mark due dates on a calendar	226	
13.	Set up tickler files	227	
14.	Read IRS notices	227	

	Strategy	Page Ref #	Application To Your Business
15.	Don't panic if you are chosen for an IRS audit	228	
16.	IRS mail audits	228	
17.	An IRS office audit	228	
18.	An IRS business location audit	228	
19.	Don't represent yourself in an audit	228	
20.	Keep good records	229	
21.	Don't just sign returns that are prepared for you	229	

CHAPTER 20
Exit Strategies & Succession Planning

Arnold has a restaurant and wants to retire in three years. He hoped that over the years that his son or daughter would want to come into the business, but they don't appear interested. How does he find a buyer, structure the sale, and access the cash tied up in his business which he will need to provide for his retirement?

Plan ahead for your exit strategy. The small business owner needs to determine their exit strategy before the time arrives to leave the business, whether voluntarily or involuntarily. It is never too early to plan for your exit strategy. You hopefully will live a normal life and have the luxury of planning and controlling your exit from the business, but you could wind up with an involuntary exit, due to death or disability. Arnold may have to plan for a longer period than three years to retire from his business.

Sell it to a family member. I believe that every parent/business owner dreams of leaving their business to their children. There is a sense of pride in providing for the next generation and keeping something that is very important to you close at hand. As a practical matter, children have minds of their own and don't always want to follow in Mom or Dad's footsteps, but may want to create their own instead. Sometimes they need to strike out on their own and come back to appreciate the business later. Sometimes they resent the business and the time that it took you away from the family as they were growing up and this may never be resolved. Making suggestions that they join you and then having them share their thoughts and desires will help determine if this is a real possibility now or in the future.

I don't recommend that children go off to college and then immediately join the family business. I believe that they need to know what it is like to work and compete in the "real" world. Sometimes parents make concessions for children in the business that unrelated employers would not. If you expect them to eventually take over the business, they need to be able to stand on their own two feet and work the hours that you do to keep the business successful. I also believe that they need to buy in and not be given the equity ownership. They need to want the business and be willing to suffer some to obtain it. Otherwise they won't fight for the business when it needs them to fight. Unfortunately Arnold's children are not interested in his business, so this is not an option for him.

Groom an employee. Bring in an employee, train them and groom them to purchase the business from you. If is in anticipation of retirement, it probably needs to be a younger employee. An employee young enough that they will be able to complete paying you and still have enough time to plan for their own retirement. You need to plan a number of years in advance to have enough time to select one or more employees to train and see if they are capable of being an owner. They must be capable of accepting the hats and responsibilities that go along with being an owner versus an employee. They should have the ability to bring some dollars to the table when the purchase time comes. Equity in a home or real estate, money borrowed from relatives, life insurance, etc. — any of this can suffice. If they don't put any of their own money or resources in the deal, they will be more likely to walk away or to give up when the going gets tough. In Arnold's case, three years is a very short time for Arnold to plan and bring someone into the business and groom them to buy him out. But he may be lucky and have someone already employed or he can begin a search for such an employee to purchase his business.

Selling the business through business brokers. There are business brokers who match up buyers and sellers. Some specialize in specific industries, others are general business brokers. They maintain databases of people wanting to sell their business and those who want to buy businesses. They will review your business financials and history and ask a number of questions and develop a marketing package, similar to a business plan that presents your business to a potential buyer in a favorable way. Many times they will discover that your financial records are not in order for a potential buyer to review. They will recommend that you work with a CPA to put your records in order. Chaos and confusion in your records makes buyers nervous and skittish about buying your business.

The broker will also value your business and make suggestions as to an asking price. There will be a broker fee, usually negotiable from five to 15% of the sales price, and will depend on the anticipated sales price of the business and the marketing efforts anticipated to sell it. The broker will negotiate the sales price with potential buyers. Make sure that the broker understands your business and can adequately represent you and your business. Ask to approve the sales material and ask for them to make a presentation to you before the business is marketed, so that you are convinced that they will do a good job for you. This may be a more realistic option for Arnold to be able to retire in three years.

Selling it on your own. It is usually difficult to represent yourself in selling your business and navigating through the negotiation process with a potential buyer. You may take the low-balling or complaints personally, instead of as part of the game.

Determining the asking price and accepting a sales price. There are a number of ways to value a business:

1) Fair market value of the assets less liabilities plus a value for goodwill,
2) Replacement value of assets less the liabilities plus a good will value,
3) Book value or stockholders' equity per the balance sheet,
4) Sales of similar businesses or comparables adjusted for your unique business,
5) Discounted cash flows of the business adjusted for expenses that that are unique to the owner, such as salary, cars, retirement plan contributions, benefits, etc.

Be realistic on value and seek outside advice. There is no deal unless you and the buyer agree on a sale price. This is a negotiation process and may be revised several times as you exchange more and more information. If the deal is meant to be, it will get worked out. It is important to keep an open mind throughout the process.

Discounted cash flows of the business. I believe that this method should be considered in all valuation computations. It doesn't matter what complicated method you arrive at, if the cash flows don't support the payments to the seller and provide a reasonable compensation level to the buyer, it won't work for all parties. You can increase the purchase price by increasing the payout period to the buyer or increasing the down payment, but the business cash flow will dictate the monthly payments available to the seller and to compensate the buyer. It doesn't work for the buyer to decide to forego a salary/compensation for a few years in order to pay more to the seller. At some point the buyer will resent the sacrifices that he or she is making to the seller and start to view the entire agreement in a negative way and conflicts could arise.

Can't count cash that was not reported on tax returns. There is a tendency for owners to pocket cash and not report it on their tax returns. Not only is this against the law, it is committing tax fraud when your tax return is filed without the income. You can't have your cake and eat it too. You can't choose to not report this income on your income tax returns and then count it when you want to sell your business. It has always amazed me that clients will keep the fact they do it a secret, until they decide to sell their business and decide that it is now okay to admit to it. It is still tax fraud and unethical. A potential buyer may decide that if you were willing to commit tax fraud, they can't trust anything else that you are representing in the sale of your business. If you want to include this unreported income, go back and file amended tax returns and pay the income tax on this income and then count it.

Compensation for sweat equity. This is your baby and your business and you probably have a fair amount of sweat equity invested from day one in the business and you want to be compensated for it. It may or may not add value to the business.

Industry valuations methods. Various industries have rules of thumb to use in valuing businesses in a particular industry. You can contact trade organizations to obtain this information. I have found executive directors very helpful with providing published articles in trade magazines and people to contact and obtain more information. By assisting you, they are protecting the industry. Industry valuation methods include but are not limited to:

1) A set number times gross revenue (i.e., 1 to 1.25)
2) A set price per customer on list of customers who have purchased services or products from the company in the last two years
3) A set number times regular, repeatable income such as rental fees

Asset sale. Most new buyers want to purchase the assets of the business and not its liabilities. The advantage of purchasing the assets outright at fair market value is that the new buyer receives a step up in basis and a new, usually higher, value to depreciate on their new books. With accelerated depreciation methods available, many small business owners have completely written off assets in the first year or years of ownership and the new owner wants to be entitled to take their deductions too. Most buyers don't want to assume stated liabilities or potential liabilities that are in the market place but have not raised their heads yet.

Goodwill. Goodwill is not very easy to value. Everyone has an opinion on how to value it. This is usually the value associated with an established business with a given clientele and reputation and quality of product or service. Goodwill value is usually determined by calculating the excess net income. This is usually done by deducting all of the ordinary and necessary business expenses from income and deducting a reasonable return on the investment in the business to the owner. This excess net income is capitalized at an investment rate of return appropriate for the risk associated with being in that particular type of business.

If the business revolves around the owner and it cannot function without the owner, then there a question that the business may not have any goodwill without the owner. The owner, in anticipation of selling the business, needs to develop systems that do not revolve around his or her presence in the business and then he or she can begin to transfer that goodwill to the company. Then it has goodwill value inside the company to sell. Certain professionals may have personal goodwill that may be able to be separately sold individually and not through the company. Please check with your tax advisor to see if you would qualify for this special treatment.

Stock sale. Very few small business sales are structured as a stock sale. The buyer cannot deduct any of the purchase prices to reduce any tax liability until the stock is ultimately sold to a third party. Along with the purchase of the stock come the assets and the actual liabilities and potential liabilities. There is usually a 'hold harmless clause' included in the purchase agreement, that states that as of the purchase date, if any more liabilities not listed in the agreement are found, the seller will hold the buyer harmless and will pay for them. If the seller still has assets to pay the new liabilities, this is great, but it is not always realistic. You can be right but not able to collect the money. Many times friendly buyers, just like family members, will be talked into a stock sale to provide the most favorable tax treatment to the seller, as will be discussed below. Unless the buyer just has to have the business, or it is valued at below fair market rate, stock sales are usually not agreeable to the buyer.

Non-compete agreements. The buyer usually doesn't want the seller to cash out and then open up down the street and compete with them and reduce the potential business income to the buyer. One way to prevent this from happening, at least for a period of time, is to structure a non-compete agreement in the sale. In order to enforce the contractual agreement there must be consideration or money paid that is declared as being in exchange for the non-compete agreement. The buyer usually wants a reasonable period of time to establish themselves with the customers and clients before the seller could potentially compete with him or her. I have seen three to 10 years with five being the most common period of time for the non-compete agreements. This is very negotiable in the sale.

Consulting agreements. The buyer usually wants access to the seller for a period of time past the closing. The initial purchase price might include a certain number of hours of transition time and after that it is a set amount per hour that the seller is paid by the buyer for consultations. No matter how careful the buyer is in including as much as possible in the purchase agreement and asking as many questions during the transition period, there will always be questions and things that were not exchanged or anticipated. The seller needs to believe that the buyer will not have an opportunity to take advantage of them and they want to be fairly compensated for their time. Additionally, the buyer needs access to them without feeling guilty for asking for the assistance.

Allocation of the sales price is required. Allocation of the sales price to the various purchased assets is required to be included in the purchase agreement so that both parties will report them the same way on their respective tax returns.

Tax consequences in the sale of your business. Under current tax laws, the general rule of the tax consequences in the sale of businesses is that if it is favorable for the buyer, it probably is not favorable for the seller, and vice versa. There is usually a compromise to meet in the middle or adjust the sales price to account for the adverse tax consequences to one or the other. Make sure that you consult with your tax advisor before agreeing to an allocation and a purchase price as you make not receive the income that you want after the taxes are paid.

Furniture, fixtures and equipment assets have ordinary and capital gain tax components. The allocation of the purchase price to the capital assets such as furniture, fixtures and equipment is treated as ordinary income to the extent depreciation was taken by the seller. This may have to be recaptured in the year of sale as ordinary income, even though it was sold on an installment method, so please check with your tax advisor to make sure enough of a down payment is obtained to pay any taxes in the first year. The amount over the original seller's purchase price of these assets will be treated as capital gains to the seller. These assets don't normally appreciate, so most of the gain is usually the recapture of the depreciation and is treated as ordinary income. The seller has ordinary income and the buyer can deduct these assets, if not in the first year with special elections, then in a fairly short period of time as an ordinary deduction against operating income.

Goodwill agreements and their tax treatment. Amounts allocated to goodwill agreements are amortizable by the buyer against ordinary income in the business over a fifteen year period. The seller will record capital gain income for the sale of goodwill.

Non-compete and consulting agreements tax treatment. Non-compete agreement payments and consulting agreement payments will be taxed as ordinary income to the seller and deductible against ordinary income over the non-compete agreement period by the buyer, or deductible to the buyer as paid under the consulting agreement.

C Corporations owning assets that are sold may cause double taxation. If a C Corporation sells assets, it will be considered the seller and will be liable for income taxes on the gains on the sale of the assets. Distributions to the owners, either through liquidation or dividends, will cause the stockholders to pay income taxes again. So consult your tax advisor to structure the deal with the least amount of tax liability.

Stock sales tax treatment. Stock sales are usually treated as long term capital gain income if the stock has been held for longer than a year by the seller. The buyer cannot deduct the sales price until he or she ultimately sells their interest in the company. There are special circumstances, such as corporate reorganizations by the buyer that may allow a reallocation of the purchase price in order for the buyer to receive more favorable tax treatment. This needs to be discussed with your tax advisor to determine if you are eligible for any of these reorganizations before the sale is finalized.

Down payments with installment payments. Most small businesses are sold with a down payment and balance paid to the seller over a number of years with interest. Banks may participate in part of the sales price if there is adequate collateral provided by the business or the seller. The Small Business Administration should be considered to assist you with obtaining a loan from a bank. The SBA and/or the bank will usually want the seller in the deal for awhile so that they have a vested interest in assisting the buyer to be successful for a period of time after the sale and loan repayment period.

Interest only for a period of time. During the transition time and until the buyer gets on their feet, the seller may consider accepting interest only payments to reduce the cash burden on the business.

Very rare to receive all cash up front. It is very rare for a seller to receive all cash up front. Again, the buyer will want the seller in the deal for awhile so that they have a vested interest in assisting the buyer to be successful for a period of time after the sale and during the loan repayment period.

Deferred compensation arrangements. Deferred compensation plans allow employees or family member/employees to use the prior earnings and current earnings of the company to buy the seller out and deduct the payments in the company against operating income. The seller will treat this income as ordinary income, but may have the annuity payments for his or her retirement under this arrangement.

Sell the business separately from the real estate. Many times the business owner has purchased or built a building for the business to own or to lease from him or her. A potential buyer may not have the resources to purchase both at the beginning. The business may be purchased first and then the building is leased to the business for a period of time until the new business owner can afford to buy the building. The leased income still provides monthly income to the seller and the building potentially could increase in value while the seller still owns it.

Request a non-disclosure agreement before releasing any records to a potential buyer. Not all potential buyers will buy your business. Make sure that you protect yourself and have each potential buyer, before any confidential information is shared, sign a non-disclosure document. This will protect you from the potential buyer using the information disclosed to compete with you or a new buyer later. You may have to sue to enforce it, but at least you have a document to enforce.

Records will be requested by the buyer to prove the financial statements. Buyers will request prior income tax returns, sales tax returns, bank statements, and overall accounting records for two to five years. Make sure that these are available upon request. You want to appear organized and prepared to sell the business and respond quickly to any buyer's request.

Involuntary leave from the business due to death or disability. You, as a business owner, need to plan for an involuntary leave from the business. Key person life and disability insurance is important for sole proprietorships as well as for small partnerships. If you or your partner is not available to run the business, the business will need to hire someone with the expertise to do this. Since the business may still need to pay you and your family and/or your partner, there should be funds available to provide for this additional person.

These insurance products provide for this potential need or catastrophe. Additional life insurance should be considered to provide for the income for your family for the rest of their life without you there to provide for them. If you have a partner, they need life insurance on your life and you on their life, to provide the money to pay your family for your interest in the business at your death. See Chapter 4, *Partnerships and Buy/Sell Agreements*, to learn more about structuring partnerships and buy/sell agreements to protect you, your family, and your business.

Where do you look for potential buyers? Assuming family members and employees are not options as buyers, there are other areas to look for qualified buyers. Advertise in the Wall Street Journal, or in local newspapers and industry trade publications. Consider merging with a competitor with the understanding that you will be bought out after the transition period. Contact a complimentary business that might provide some synergies with your business as part of their product offerings. Let your business associates and sales representatives that visit you on a regular basis know that you looking for a partner or buyer. They may be able to match you up with someone who is looking too.

Don't wait until the last minute. The bottom line is that you as an owner need to plan ahead. Don't wait until the last minute to determine your successor. Your needs and desires may change over the life of your business. It is OK to change your mind along the way. Your business is usually one of your biggest assets and you need to protect the future of this asset, so that it can continue to provide the bread and butter for you and your family.

Arnold should consider all of these options and begin to plan immediately and work toward retirement, but he might have to accept a longer period before he can retire.

EXIT STRATEGIES & SUCCESSION PLANNING CHECKLIST

	Strategy	Page Ref #	Application To Your Business
1.	Plan ahead for your exit strategy	233	
2.	Sell it to a family member as possible	233	
3.	Groom an employee	234	
4.	Selling the business through business brokers	234	
5.	Selling it on your own	235	
6.	Determining the asking price and accepting a sales price	235	
7.	Discounted cash flows of the business	236	
8.	Can't count cash that was not reported on tax returns	236	
9.	Compensation for sweat equity	236	
10.	Industry valuations methods	237	
11.	Asset sale	237	
12.	Goodwill	237	
13.	Stock sale	238	

	Strategy	Page Ref #	Application To Your Business
14.	Non-compete agreements	238	
15.	Consulting agreements	238	
16.	Allocation of the sales price is required	239	
17.	Tax consequences in the sale of your business	239	
18.	Furniture, fixtures and equipment assets have ordinary and capital gain tax components	239	
19.	Goodwill agreements and their tax treatment	240	
20.	Non-compete and consulting agreements tax treatment	240	
21.	C-Corporations owning assets that are sold may cause double taxation	240	
22.	Stock sales tax treatment	240	
23.	Down payments with installment payments	240	
24.	Interest only for a period of time	240	
25.	Very rare to receive all cash up front	241	
26.	Deferred compensation arrangements	241	

	Strategy	Page Ref #	Application To Your Business
27.	Sell the business separately from the real estate	241	
28.	Request a non-disclosure agreement before releasing any records to a potential buyer	241	
29.	Records will be requested by the buyer to prove the financial statements	241	
30.	Involuntary leave from the business due to death or disability	242	
31.	Where do you look for potential buyers?	242	
32.	Don't wait until the last minute	242	

APPENDIX A
New Business Checklist

1. Develop Concept
2. Develop Business Plan
3. Develop Budget
4. Choose Professional Team
    a. CPA
    b. Lawyer
    c. Banker
    d. Insurance Professional
5. Choose Name
6. Obtain Domain Name
7. Choose Legal Entity
8. Form Entity
9. Apply for Federal Identification Number
10. File S Corporation Election if applicable

11. Develop and sign Buy/Sell Agreements

12. Open Bank Account

13. Choose Business Location

14. Raise Capital

15. Negotiate Lease

16. Obtain phone, fax and toll-free numbers

17. Obtain business license

18. Obtain insurance
    a. Property and Casualty
    b. General Liability
    c. Workman's Compensation
    d. Errors and Omissions
    e. Group Health
    f. Group Disability
    g. Group Long Term Care
    h. Key Person Life

19. Furniture, Fixtures and Equipment
    a. Determine needs:
        i. Furniture
        ii. Fax Machines
        iii. Copy Machines

iv. Postage Machine

b. Obtain financing

c. Purchase

20. Employees

a. Develop employee manual

b. Develop training programs

c. Hire Employees

21. Technology

a. Software

i. Database/Customer Relationship Manager

ii. Accounting System

iii. Inventory

iv. Word Processing

v. Email

vi. Point of Sale

vii. Industry specific

b. Hardware

i. Server

ii. Workstations

iii. Laptops

iv. Docking Stations

v. PDA

vi. Fax server

vii. Email server

viii. Printers

ix. Backup

x. Battery backup

22. Obtain Email addresses

23. Develop procedures for maintaining Database

24. Develop logo and theme for marketing materials

25. Trademark logos

26. Develop marketing plan

27. Print marketing materials

    a. Business cards

    b. Letterhead and envelopes

    c. Brochures

28. Develop website

29. Develop Internet marketing plan

30. Establish Accounting Systems

    a. Cash

    b. Accounts Receivable

    c. Accounts Payable

    d. Inventory

    e. Opening Mail

31. Establish procedures for Managing Cash Flow
    a. Daily reports
    b. Weekly reports
    c. Monthly reports
    d. Updating Budgets

32. Establish procedures of Inventory
    a. Purchasing
    b. Pricing
    c. Fulfilling orders
    d. Re-order points
    e. Purchase Orders
    f. Ordering
    g. Sales
    h. Obsolescence

APPENDIX B
Budget Sample

DESCRIPTIONS	Budget	% of Income
Income		
Product A		
Product B		
Product C		
Product D		
Total Income		
Cost of Goods Sold		
Materials		
Labor		
Other expenses		
Total Cost of Goods Sold		

DESCRIPTIONS	Budget	% of Income
Gross Profit		
Selling Expenses		
Commissions		
Travel for Sales Reps		
Credit Card / Merchant Services		
Shipping out		
Total Selling Expenses		
General Expenses		
Advertising		
Books and publications		
Dues and subscriptions		
Insurance		
Group health		
Liability		
Workman's Compensation		
Fire and Theft		

DESCRIPTIONS	Budget	% of Income
Key person life insurance		
Interest		
Legal services		
Licenses		
Meals and entertainment		
Office supplies		
Postage		
Printing and reproduction		
Rent		
Repairs and Maintenance		
Seminars and education		
Taxes		
Payroll taxes		
Property taxes		
Telephone		
Office lines		
Cell phones		

DESCRIPTIONS	Budget	% of Income
Travel		
Wages		
Officers		
Office Staff		
Field Staff		
Other Staff		
Total General Expenses		
Net Income Before Taxes		
Income Taxes		
Net Income		

APPENDIX C
Internet Resources

RUN A SUCCESSFUL BUSINESS RESOURCES

www.RunASuccessfulBusiness.com

TAX UPDATES

www.RunASuccessfulBusiness.com

ACCOUNTING SOFTWARE

QuickBooks
www.QuickBooks.com

Microsoft Small Business Accounting
www.OfficeSmallBusinessAccounting.com

CERTIFIED PUBLIC ACCOUNTANT

Strategic Business Resources, Inc.
www.SpringerCPA.com

FINANCIAL SERVICES

Legacy Wealth Management, Inc.
www.LegacyWMI.com

DATABASE SOFTWARE

Act 2006

www.Act.com

Microsoft Dynamics CRM

www.Microsoft.com/dynamics

TECHNOLOGY

Dell Computer

www.Dell.com/smallbusiness

Compaq

www.Compaq.com

Hewlett Packard

http://hp.com

Symantec Anti-Virus Research Center (SARC)

(read up on latest vial threats)

www.SARC.com

INTERNET TECHNOLOGY CONSULTANT

Carceron Systems Group, LLC

http://Carceron.net

MARKETING & INTERNET MARKETING

GoDaddy.com — Doman Names

www.GoDaddy.com

GRAPHIC DESIGN, COLOR PRINTING, WEBSITES & AD SPECIALTIES

Big Dawg Prints
www.BigDawgPrints.com

East Cobb Printing
www.EastCobbPrinting.com

WEBSITE APPLICATION & SOFTWARE DEVELOPMENT

SLK Ware.Com
www.SLKWare.com

OFFICE FURNITURE & LAYOUT

Kennesaw Office Interiors
www.KennesawOffice.com

TELEPHONY, VOICE AND DATA

Elite Telecom Services — Vendor Neutral Telecom & ISP Broker
www.EliteSvc.com

BUSINESS PLAN PRO SOFTWARE

www.BusinessPlanPro.com

HUMAN RESOURCES

Applicant Skill & Personality Assessment Testing
www.BrainBench.com
www.Injoy.com

Employee Manual Software
www.SampleEmployeeHandbook.com
www.CertifiedEmployeeHandbook.com

GOVERNMENT

Internal Revenue Service (IRS)
www.IRS.gov

Small Business Administration (SBA)
http://SBA.gov

ORGANIZATIONS

American Institute of Certified Public Accountants (AICPA)
www.AICPA.org

National Association of Insurance and Financial Association (NAIFA)
http://NAIFA.org

American Bar Association (ABA)
www.ABAnet.org

OTHER RESOURCES

Microsoft Small Business Center
www.Microsoft.com/smallbusiness

Microsoft Office Training & Resource
http://Office.Microsoft.com

Business Publications Search Engine
www.BPubs.com

SCORE — Resource Partner for the SBA, Counselors to Small Business
(free business guide CD or available for download)
www.Score.org

APPENDIX D
Retirement Plans

2006 LIMITS

Type of Retirement Plan	2006 Maximum Contributions	2006 Catch up if over 50
Individual Retirement Plan Traditional IRA(*)	$4,000	$1,000
Individual Retirement Plan Roth IRA (*)	$4,000	$1,000
Simplified Employee Pension (SEP) Plan	$44,000	
Savings Incentive Match for Employees (Simple) Plan	$10,000	$2,500
Profit Sharing Plan	$44,000	
Comparability Profit Sharing Plan	$44,000	
Defined Benefit Plan	Wage Limit to 100% of compensation to a maximum of $175,000	

Type of Retirement Plan	2006 Maximum Contributions	2006 Catch up if over 50
401-(k) Plan	$15,000	$5,000
Safe Harbor 401 (k) Plan	$15,000	$5,000
Individual (k) Plan	$44,000	

(*) May be limited if you or your spouse are covered under an employer plan

Please note that tax updated information for future years can be downloaded from RunASuccessfulBusiness.com. Visit this website for more resources for a successful business.

2007 LIMITS

Type of Retirement Plan	2007 Maximum Contributions	2007 Catch up if over 50
Individual Retirement Plan Traditional IRA(*)	$4,000	$1,000
Individual Retirement Plan Roth IRA (*)	$4,000	$1,000
Simplified Employee Pension (SEP) Plan	$45,000	
Savings Incentive Match for Employees (Simple) Plan	$10,500	$2,500
Profit Sharing Plan	$45,000	
Comparability Profit Sharing Plan	$45,000	
Defined Benefit Plan	Wage Limit to 100% of compensation to a maximum of $180,000	
401-(k) Plan	$15,500	$5,000
Safe Harbor 401 (k) Plan	$15,500	$5,000
Individual (k) Plan	$45,000	

(*) May be limited if you or your spouse are covered under an employer plan

Please note that tax updated information for future years can be downloaded from RunASuccessfulBusiness.com. Visit this website for more resources for a successful business.

ABOUT THE AUTHOR
Ellen V. Springer
MBA, AEP, CLTC, CSA, RFC, CPA

Ellen V. Springer has over 25 years experience in business and financial consulting and is committed to sharing her expertise with the business community, individuals, and organizations.

Marketing
Employees
Cash Flow

She has founded, built, and sold two traditional CPA practices in the last 20 years. Responsibilities included general management, marketing and public relations, client acquisitions, business system development, and staffing and training of personnel. She is currently Managing Director and Principle for Legacy Wealth Management, Inc. and President of her public accounting firm, Strategic Business Resources, Inc.

In addition to managing her companies, Ellen is an adjunct Professor of Business at Kennesaw State University and Mercer University, and a National Instructor for The Corporation for Long Term Care Certification, Inc. (CLTC). She is frequently sought after as a speaker on business, financial, and tax issues for conventions, organizations and businesses.

As a community leader, Ellen has served on numerous boards, including Chambers of Commerce, cities, and corporations. She is currently the Board Chair of the YWCA of Northwest Georgia, Treasurer of Kennesaw Business Association, Treasurer of Visions Anew Institute, Board Member of the Coles Business School of Kennesaw State University, Board Member of the WellStar

Foundation, Past President of the Georgia Society of CPA's North Atlanta Chapter, and Past President of the Estate Planning Council of North Georgia.

In 2006, Ellen received the Women Entrepreneur (WE) Inspiration Award, by National Association of Women Business Owners (NAWBO) and Georgia Women Entrepreneur Network (GWEN). In 2005, Ellen was recognized as the "Kennesaw Citizen of the Year" by the Cobb Chamber of Commerce and in 2003 received the "President's Award" from the Kennesaw Business Association. She has been honored as a Woman of Achievement by the YWCA.

She has a BSBA in Business Administration from the University of South Florida and a MBA from Georgia State University, has raised two children, and currently lives in Kennesaw, Georgia.

About This Book

So, you consider yourself blessed with a certain "entrepreneurial streak" and you are either considering starting-up a business or have already done so and are passionate about it succeeding! Or... maybe you just want to help change some of the more bizarre functions within your company and want to be a "causative force" involved in this change?!

The book that you are holding is a plain English explanation by topic and a treasure map for telling you exactly how to keep from getting blown-away as you traverse all the proverbial "business minefields"! Now, look again at the back cover under "Topics/Chapters". As you read those 20 Topics, you should start to recognize that Ellen Springer, a CPA that has consulted for over 25 years with small business owners and has started, grown, and then sold her own successful businesses, has written these Chapters from the perspective of "been there... done that...!" She is definitely a Dean at the "School of Hard Knocks"...

One other thing; Yes, this book is an exemplary business reference on "what to do and not do", but if you look again at the order of the Chapters, they do follow and flow through the actual life cycle of a business. And, at the end of each Chapter, there is a "Checklist" that helps you summarize all the information and neat ideas she has just given you and a space to write down how to apply the idea to your business. Additionally, at the end of the book are four "Appendices" that provide you with Worksheets, Samples, Plans, Resources, etc., etc.

Turning Your Dream Business Into Your Bread & Butter, Recipes for Running a Successful Business From Scratch is a must for any business owner that wants to be successful!

Visit www.RunASuccessfulBusiness.com for more resources on how to run a successful business.

IMPROVE THE QUALITY OF YOUR LIFE

Most business owners, at one time or another, become overwhelmed with the management of their business.

Ellen would like to help you with her Audio Recording and PowerPoint Slides entitled *"How to Improve the Quality of YOUR Life by Taking Care of THE Business."* Listen to Ellen V. Springer as she reveals these invaluable strategies to "Improve the Quality of YOUR Life." You will:

- Learn about your most precious resource
- Find "less" time to accomplish more
- Increase Cash Flow
- Work Smarter, Not Harder

Download your BONUS Audio Recording and PowerPoint Slides — a $97 Value — at:

www.RunASuccessfulBusiness.com

Turning Your Dream Business Into Your Bread & Butter Audio Book

Yes/No

_______ Do you want to listen to the chapter that you need for your business when you need it?

_______ Don't have time to read the book but want the information as soon as possible?

_______ Do you learn better by listening rather than reading?

If you answered "Yes" to any of these questions, the Audio Book is your answer.

Ask your bookstore or visit

www.RunASuccessfulBusiness.com

for information to purchase the Audio Book and other resources to run your business more successfully.

Printed in the United States
77669LV00002B/81-108

9 781600 372230